UNITED NATIONS CONFERENCE ON TRADE AND DEVELOPMENT

UNCTAD

HARNESSING BLOCKCHAIN FOR SUSTAINABLE DEVELOPMENT: PROSPECTS AND CHALLENGES

UNITED NATIONS
Geneva, 2021

This publication has not been formally edited.

United Nations publication issued by the United Nations Conference on Trade and Development.

UNCTAD/DTL/STICT/2021/3

ISBN: 978-92-1-113020-1
eISBN: 978-92-1-403043-0
Sales No.: E.21.II.D.16

ACKNOWLEDGEMENTS

This study was prepared by an UNCTAD team, comprised of Clovis Freire (team leader), Abiy Solomon, Maria Godunova, Weijing Ye and Ronak Shahsavar, with contributions from Solomon Anzagra, Thomas Van Giffen, Olivier Combe and Rasim Alam (Harvard Kennedy School). The authors worked under the supervision of Liping Zhang, Chief of the Science, Technology and Innovation Policy Section, and the guidance of Ángel González Sanz, Head of the Science, Technology and ICT Branch, and under the overall direction of Shamika N. Sirimanne, Director of the UNCTAD Division on Technology and Logistics.

UNCTAD appreciates valuable inputs provided by the Governments of Austria, Belgium, Cuba, Finland, the Islamic Republic of Iran, Kenya, Latvia, Portugal, Romania, the Russian Federation, Saudi Arabia, Switzerland, Thailand, Turkey and the United Kingdom of Great Britain and Northern Ireland, as well as from United Nations Economic and Social Commission for Asia (ESCAP), United Nations Economic and Social Commission for Western Asia (ESCWA), Food and Agriculture Organization of the United Nations (FAO), International Trade Centre (ITC), Food and Agriculture Organization (ITU), United Nations Economic Commission for Europe (UNECE), United Nations Industrial Development Organization (UNIDO), United Nations World Food Programme (WFP) and World Intellectual Property Organization (WIPO).

The publication benefited significantly from discussions and inputs during the 2020–2021 Intersessional Panel of the United Nations Commission on Science and Technology for Development (18 to 22 January 2021).

Magali Studer designed the cover. Malou Pasinos provided administrative support.

NOTE

The United Nations Conference on Trade and Development (UNCTAD) serves as the lead entity within the United Nations Secretariat for matters related to science and technology as part of its work on the integrated treatment of trade and development, investment and finance. The current UNCTAD work programme is based on the mandates set at quadrennial conferences, as well as on the decisions of the General Assembly of the United Nations and the United Nations Economic and Social Council that draw upon the recommendations of the United Nations Commission on Science and Technology for Development, which is served by the UNCTAD secretariat. The UNCTAD work programme is built on its three pillars of research analysis, consensus-building and technical cooperation, and is carried out through intergovernmental deliberations, research and analysis, technical assistance activities, seminars, workshops and conferences.

This series of publications seeks to contribute to exploring current issues in science, technology, and innovation, with particular emphasis on their impact on developing countries.

CONTENTS

LIST OF BOXES

LIST OF FIGURES

LIST OF TABLES

I. INTRODUCTION

In an increasingly digitalized economy and society, the security and accountability of data transactions are critical elements for creating trust and enabling breakthrough innovations in the digital world. In this regard, blockchain technology could be a game-changer, with the potential to revolutionize processes from finance to pharmaceutical industries, from government public services to humanitarian work and development aid. The blockchain serves as the base technology for cryptocurrency, enabling open (peer-to-peer), secure and fast transactions. The blockchain application has expanded to include various financial transactions (e.g., online payments and exchange platforms), Internet of things (IoT), health systems and supply chains.

However, issues associated with scalability, privacy concerns, uncertain regulatory standards and difficulties posed by technology integration with existing applications are some of the potential market constraints. There is also the risk that the potential of blockchain for solving developmental problems has been somewhat inflated by its early adopters and the technology media and may not be as applicable for developing and least developed countries.

What are the emerging uses of blockchain that can be breakthroughs in accelerating progress towards Sustainable Development Goals? What are the potential adverse unintended social and economic effects of this technology? How could Governments maximize the opportunities and minimize the risks?

The paper's main messages are that blockchain technology can be used in many applications that could contribute to sustainable development. However, at this moment, blockchain innovation has focused on financial applications dissociated from the real economy. For most of the innovations in this field, the Goal is to profit by extracting rents through financial intermediation and speculative gains in cryptofinancial assets instead of creating real value through new products and services. Such behaviour, combined with the lack of regulation and the swift pace of innovation, is a receipt for financial bubbles and bursts.

At the same time, blockchain is potentially a key technology in a new technological paradigm of increasing automation and integrating physical and virtual worlds, together with technologies such as artificial intelligence (AI), robots, and gene editing. In such a scenario of the very early stages of this new paradigm's installation period, it is still not clear the real long-impact of these technologies on the economy, societies and environment. Similar moments in the past technological revolutions offered windows of opportunity for some developing countries to catch up and others to forge ahead. Therefore, Governments of developing countries should seek to strengthen their innovation systems to strategically position themselves to benefit from this new wave of technological change.

The paper is structured as follows. Chapter II sets the stage by briefly presenting blockchain technology. Chapter III discusses the ecosystem of innovation related to blockchain technologies. It discusses the types of blockchain innovation, main actors, networks and interlinkages that they form to exchange knowledge, learn and innovate. Chapter IV discusses how blockchain could impact the Sustainable Development Goals, focusing on how possible scenarios could play out and their effect on sustainable development. Chapter V discusses the challenges that Governments face and what they could do to influence the rate and direction of innovation and competence building in blockchain to contribute to their national development priorities and accelerate the progress towards the Sustainable Development Goals. And chapter VI discusses areas for international collaboration.

II. THE BLOCKCHAIN TECHNOLOGY

A. WHAT IS BLOCKCHAIN?

Blockchain technology was invented to create Bitcoin. Introduced to the world in 2008, in a White Paper titled "Bitcoin: A Peer-to-Peer Electronic Cash System" published under the pseudonym Satoshi Nakamoto, whose true identity has never been revealed, bitcoin is defined as "a purely peer-to-peer version of electronic cash [that] would allow online payments to be sent directly from one party to another without going through a financial institution" (Nakamoto, 2008). The stated Goal of Bitcoin was to reduce transaction costs, fraud and payment uncertainties in digital transactions. It was proposed as an alternative to the prevalent model of e-commerce that relies on financial institutions serving as trusted third parties to process electronic payments.

Therefore, the technical problem that blockchain technology was invented to solve was creating a ledger (register of payments) online without a central node that has control over the information in the ledger. One of the Bitcoin protocol's security concerns is the double-spending problem; a person spending the same Bitcoin more than once. Blockchain solves that problem in a distributed ledger through an ingenious combination of blocks of data, cryptography and an algorithm for network nodes to reach a consensus about the ledger's transactions, the proof-of-work (PoW) consensus distribution algorithm (see box 1).

Being a digital asset without any intrinsic value and central controller or issuer, Bitcoin is regarded as ground-breaking in the evolution of fiat currencies (BIS, 2020). It laid the foundations of blockchain technology and enabled the development of other cryptocurrencies. These other cryptocurrencies are implemented using variations of blockchain, which can differ substantially from the way that Satoshi Nakamoto initially proposed it. Thus, many prefer to use the more general term Distributed Ledger Technologies (DLT) when referring to other blockchain implementations. In this paper, both terms are used interchangeably. A list of terms related to the blockchain is presented in the blockchain glossary in the annex to this publication.

An example of the variations in the implementation of blockchain is related to the network's management and permissions, which divides blockchains into two basic categories: public and private blockchains. A public (or permissionless) blockchain is one where anyone can read all transactions taking place, and anyone can participate in the network and help maintain the ledger. Bitcoin is implemented in a public blockchain. In a private (or permissioned) blockchain, both the information and maintenance of the network are restricted to a selected group of known participants. Private ledger technology is typically applied in enterprise use cases where immutable transactions are required and can be verified only by a few nodes (United Nations/CEFACT, 2020).

While the Bitcoin network only records transactions of cryptocurrency, second-generation blockchains (Blockchain 2.0) expand it by allowing the record of computer code in the ledger (figure 1). It is like creating a distributed hard drive that stores computer code that can be executed in the nodes of the network. Thus, for instance, instead of only registering that a payment has been made, the blockchain can store "smart contracts" that are executed automatically when their conditions are met. The incorporation of smart contracts enables business functions involving the transfer of information and value while leaving transparent and reliably auditable information trails (United Nations/CEFACT, 2020).

Smart contracts were first implemented in a platform called Ethereum, an open-source distributed computing platform featuring smart contracts for decentralized applications (DApps). The idea of Ethereum was introduced in 2013 in a White Paper titled "A Next-Generation Smart Contract and Decentralized Application Platform" released by Vitalik Buterin, a then 19-year-old Russian–Canadian programmer. Buterin proposed the development of a new platform "allowing anyone to write smart contracts and decentralized applications where they can create their own arbitrary rules for ownership, transaction formats and state transition functions" (Buterin, 2013) (see box 2 for more information regarding Ethereum). The blockchain is called Ethereum and Ether (ETH) is the cryptocurrency token generated by Ethereum miners as a reward for computations performed to secure the blockchain. In October 2020, Ethereum was the second-largest cryptocurrency platform by market capitalization, behind Bitcoin.[1]

[1] See https://www.blockchain.com.

Box 1
How blockchain works

When a node in a network makes or receives payments from another node, it sends the information about this transaction to all other nodes in the network. This information basically says that payment of value X was made from node A to node B at a specific time. That transaction is then registered in the distributed ledger by a third node, which is called a miner, who verifies the validity of the transaction by solving a very complex computational math problem.

Transactions are registered in blocks, many transactions at a time. Given that these blocks of transactions can be created by different nodes in the network, a new block must somehow be connected to the previous blocks. In a blockchain, each new block is "chained" to the previous blocks using a cryptographic signature. This signature is easy to verify but extremely difficult to replicate. It is created using a cryptographic technique called hashing, which takes large amounts of data as input and creates a unique identifier known as the "hash value" or "digital fingerprint". With hashing, it is impossible to recreate the data that generated the hash value.

Nodes that generate new blocks are called miners because they are rewarded with newly created (mined) bitcoins for the trouble of generating a new block of transactions. Given that more than one miner in the network can create a new block using this technique, a consensus mechanism is used to select which potential new block is considered by all participants as the "agreed" new block of transactions in the blockchain. Bitcoin uses a proof-of-work (PoW) consensus distribution algorithm, in which each node that generates a new block must prove that it has worked in a cryptographic challenge. The challenge is to generate a hash value of the blockchain with a sequence of zeros of a certain length at the beginning (e.g., 19 zeros). This is not an easy task, and miners must try different ways of combining transactions in a block, adding strings of data to the block to try to create the hash with leading zeros. The difficulty of this challenge is set by the blockchain algorithm, based on the number of transactions and nodes, so that a new block is generated on average every 10 minutes regardless of the number of transactions, nodes, or computer power used for mining. If two nodes solve this challenge, the node that generated the longer blockchain is considered by all other nodes as the one that has created the new block in the blockchain.

One of the threats to the blockchain is the Sybil or 51 per cent attack, which occurs when a malevolent actor controls a majority of the nodes, then it could decide to reach a consensus in contradiction of the interests of other participants of the network.

Source: UNCTAD, based on Nakamoto (2008) and United Nations Innovation Network (2019).

The latest technological advances in blockchain are clustered around what could be called Blockchain 3.0, which focus on addressing the drawbacks of the previous two generations of blockchain technology, such as scalability and interoperability between different blockchains (Ackermann and Meier, 2018). For example, blockchain can potentially support most of the applications of Industry 4.0 including supply chain and trade across manufacturing, food, pharmaceutical, health and creative industries through integrating varied systems, managing commercial transactions and fostering the assets' traceability (Bodkhe et al., 2020). However, some technical limitations of Bitcoin and Ethereum such as high transaction fees and limited scalability, prevent blockchain's first two generations from a general application within Industry 4.0. Blockchain 3.0 is comprised of blockchain innovations to enable fast, large-scale applications. For example, one of the innovations is the proof-of-stake (PoS) protocol, the consensus distribution algorithm in which the eligibility of creating a new block is determined by the amount a node has invested in the network. This innovation reduces the time required for the creation of a new block, increasing the performance of the applications.

Figure 1
The evolution of blockchain

Cryptocurrency

- The foundation of blockchain technologies
- Cryptocurrency blockchains
- Peer-to-peer decentralised cryptocurrency transactions
- Proof-of-work (PoW) protocol

BLOCKCHAIN 1.0

Smart Contracts

- More financial functionality than simply being a cryptocurrency transactions processor
- Decentralized applications (DApps) based on programmable language
- Autonomously executing algorithms
- Proof-of-work (PoW) protocol

BLOCKCHAIN 2.0

More Functionality

- Larger-scale of applications of non cryptocurrency-related Distributed Ledger Technology (DLT)
- Improved performance with more scalability and interoperability
- Proof-of-stake (PoS) protocol

BLOCKCHAIN 3.0

Source: UNCTAD.

Box 2
Ethereum

Ethereum can be considered as a distributed computer, the Ethereum Virtual Machine (EVM). The Ethereum protocol keeps the EVM running (Ethereum Virtual Machine (EVM), 2020). The EVM begins with an initial state and continuously execute transactions to morph it into the current state. It is this current state that is accepted as the canonical "version" of the world of Ethereum, and at any given block in the chain, Ethereum has only one 'canonical' state. The state can include any information that can be represented by a computer such as account balances and trust arrangements (Wood, 2020).

Each transaction on Ethereum requires computational resources to execute; thus, each transaction requires a fee. The term "Gas" refers to the unit that measures the amount of computational effort required to execute specific transactions on the Ethereum network successfully. Gas fees are paid in Ether, and its prices are denoted in Gwei, which itself is a denomination of Ether: each Gwei is equal to 0.000000001 ETH. The price of the gas is determined by the demand for resources on the network; the amount of gas depends on the computational efforts needed and the time to execute a transaction. Miners can decline to process a transaction if the gas price does not meet their threshold. Requiring a fee for every transaction executed on the network helps prevent actors from spamming the network. The reason for introducing gas as a distinct value or separate unit than Ether is to maintain a distinction between the actual valuation of the cryptocurrency and the computational expenses on the Ethereum network (Ethereum: Gas and fees, 2020).

In 2016, US$50 million in Ether was stolen by an anonymous hacker. To return the amount stolen to their rightful owners, the Ethereum platform was divided (forked) into two versions: the new version became Ethereum (ETH), and the original chain, Ethereum Classic (ETC) (Waters, 2016). The Ethereum Foundation (EF) is the organization dedicated to supporting Ethereum and related technologies. It is a non-profit organization based in Switzerland with the mission to contribute to Ethereum's long-term success by promoting and supporting Ethereum-related technologies' research, development, and community. Ethereum Foundation's reported role is not to control Ethereum, but to allocate resources, both financial and non-financial, to critical projects, to be a valued voice within the Ethereum ecosystem and to advocate for Ethereum to the outside world (Ethereum Foundation, 2020).

Source: UNCTAD.

B. APPLICATIONS, STATUS AND TRENDS

According to some estimates, the market for blockchain solutions and applications was around US$708 million in 2017, and it is expected to reach over US$60 billion in 2024 (MarketWatch, 2019). Blockchain can be used in virtually any application. Currently, the prominent use cases for blockchain applications are in the areas of online payments, finance, international trade, and global value chains. In the demand side, the growth of blockchain market is mainly driven by factors such as increasing online transactions, digitization of currency, secure online payment gateways, the growing interest of the banking, financial services and insurance sector, and an increasing number of merchants accepting cryptocurrencies (Grand View Research, 2019).

1. Cryptocurrencies, tokens and online payments

The first and probably the best-known application of blockchain technology is to build online payment systems with fast, cheap and secure transactions and without intermediaries. There are many projects in this space, such as Bitcoin, Litecoin, EOS, NEO, Ripple, Dash, and more recently, Facebook's Libra. In addition to cryptocurrencies such as Bitcoin and Monero, they also include protocol tokens (e.g. Ether), utility tokens, securities tokens (e.g. cryptoequities, cryptobonds), natural asset tokens, cryptofiat currencies and stablecoins (for a discussion on the advantages and disadvantages of cryptocurrencies as opposed to other forms of currency, traditional or digital, see chapter IV).

In October 2020, there were about 1,000 cryptocurrencies in the market. This number was lower than in 2018 when there were more than 1,500. Many still have a negligible market capitalization (figure 2). Only 17 have a market capitalization of more than US$1 billion and 46 have a market capitalization higher than US$100 million. The total capitalization of the 100 most valued cryptocurrencies is about US$330 billion, in which Bitcoin accounts for US$200 billion (CoinMarketCap, 2020).

Figure 2
Market shares of cryptocurrencies, October 2020
(Percentage)

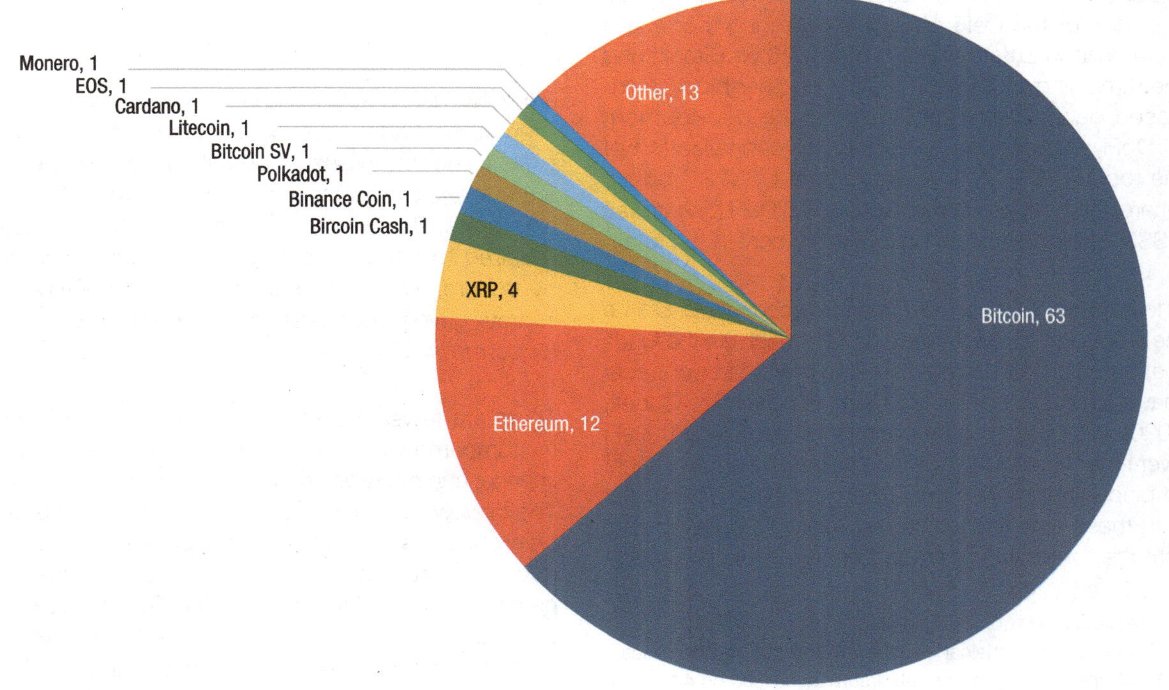

Source: UNCTAD, based on coinmarketcap.com.
Note: "Other" represents more than 1,000 other cryptocurrencies exchanged in October 2020.

In terms of transactions, in October 2020, the number of Bitcoin transactions per day was about 300 thousand,[2] while, for comparison, the credit card company Visa handles more than 65,000 transactions per second, which is more than 5.6 trillion transactions per day (Visa, 2018). In 2018 there were 460 million Bitcoins wallets in total with only 25 million wallets holding bitcoins,[3] while there were 3.3 billion Visa cards worldwide in the same period (Visa, 2018).

2. Decentralized finance

Decentralized finance (DeFi) is currently the area with a great amount of innovation. DeFi refers to blockchain-based financial instruments run by smart contracts – which automatically execute transactions if certain conditions are met - that expand the use of blockchain from simple value transfer to more complex financial use cases without any intermediaries. For instance, if a user wants her money to be sent to another user next Tuesday, but only if the US$/EUR exchange rate is higher than 0,85 according to xe.com, such if-else or if-then instructions can be embedded in smart contracts. Applications use smart contracts in platforms such as Ethereum to create currency exchanges, yield farms, microcredit applications, insurance, etc.

In November 2020, there were 251 DeFi projects listed in DeFiprime.com, a media outlet and analytical services provider for the DeFi community. Among them, 203 were built on Ethereum blockchain, 26 on Bitcoin and the remaining 22 built on EOS – another blockchain-based decentralized platform for the development of DeFi applications.[4] The market capitalization of the top 100 DeFi tokens was about US$12.7 billion, wherein the market value of the top 10 DeFi tokens was US$9.1 billion, accounting for 71 per cent of the total.[5]

Another relevant measure of market prospects for DeFi is the amount of "locked" funds in DeFi, which are the funds that users have trusted to send to the smart contracts that sustain the DeFi ecosystem. (ConsenSys Codefi, 2020). An increasing amount of locked funds in DeFi over time represents growing confidence among users to place their money into smart contracts to interact with these new financial tools. Available data indicate that the total value of funds locked in DeFi projects is in continuous and steady growth; the current value is about US$11.06 billion, and the top 10 DeFi projects represent 94 per cent of the total (figure 3).[6]

Figure 3
Share of total funds locked in DeFi, by DeFi project
(Percentage)

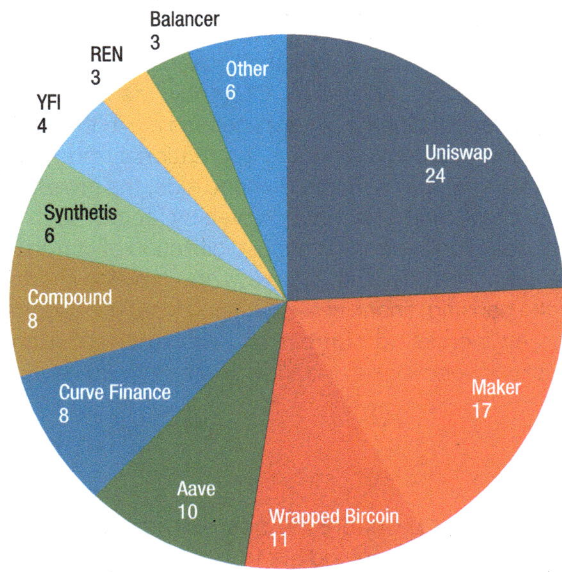

Source: UNCTAD, based on data retrieved from defipulse.com

3. International trade

Blockchain technology could improve nearly all aspects of international trade. Smart contracts allow for automatic, speedy, and timely issuance of customs invoices, permits, licences and certificates triggered after payments of fees and duties. This could cut down the back-office duties required to ensure reconciliation of duty payments by traders, reduce consignment clearance time and improve government revenues by reducing the potential for corruption.

There are fewer blockchain applications in this area as compared with online payments and decentralized finance, and many are in the stage of proof-of-concept. They involve complex procedures such as customs clearance, as well as several operations, types of documents and many stakeholders such as customs, partner governmental agencies (PGAs), customs brokers, carriers, banks, insurance companies (see box 3 for further information on the context of the UNCTAD Automated System for Customs Data – ASYCUDA).

2 See https://www.blockchain.com.

3 See https://blog.chainalysis.com/reports/bitcoin-addresses.

4 See https://defiprime.com/ethereum (accessed on 4 November 2020).

5 See https://coinmarketcap.com/defi/ (accessed on 16 October 2020).

6 See https://defipulse.com (accessed on 16 October 2020).

Box 3
ASYCUDA and blockchain

International trade more and more considers blockchain to ensure secure, trustworthy services and information exchange without costly intermediation. Customs clearance and single window systems that connect several trade stakeholders (ministries, cross-border regulatory agencies, government agencies) and exchange information with other systems (e.g. customs clearance systems for regional transit monitoring) would benefit from blockchain and the ASYCUDA programme has started to work on several practical applications.

Within the context of process automation and procedure streamlining, a blockchain acts as a process coordinator improving efficiency. With the implementation of smart contracts, secure transactions can be executed automatically in the blockchain. In a complex procedure such as customs clearance that involves several operations, types of documents, many stakeholders such as customs, partner governmental agencies (PGAs), customs brokers, carriers, banks and insurance companies, reducing unnecessary human action through smart contracts would allow faster execution and automatic compliance with rules and laws; leading to more automation, fewer corruption thanks to less human interaction (Sustainable Development Goal 16), and further implementation of paperless processes (Sustainable Development Goal 15).

In the context of the COVID-19 pandemic, these benefits can contribute to the risk mitigation efforts and measures. The payment of taxes is a great example of how blockchain and smart contracts can help; the same approach can be used for the release of guarantee after a transit procedure is completed or for the transfer of the ownership of goods in a warehouse. Not only the payment of taxes could be more secure (data cannot be corrupted) and instantaneous, but it could also be automatically executed once a declaration is registered in the system without any further human action required. Blockchain may also improve risk management, ensuring the integrity of permits, licenses and certificates and, consequently, of the value of the goods. Verification of goods could be shortened, and more efficient (Sustainable Development Goal 6) and the accurate and timely collection of taxes and duties achieved (Sustainable Development Goal 1). Combining the blockchain with another technology like IoT could be of particular interest when it comes to risk management. For instance, it can shorten the time of examination of a container thanks to the tracking of movements, temperature and opening of doors. For food, this combination guarantees security and safety, directly contributing to Sustainable Development Goals 2 and 3.

Developing countries, where efficiency and trust are low, can benefit the most from blockchains. However, the technical infrastructure needs to be assessed and the system requirements specified for a technical upgrade where appropriate, which can be pricey, especially for economies with limited financial resources such as LDCs. In that context, many member States will seek financing from donors, making donor coordination a key aspect to success. The capacity-building component will be more important and complex in the context of a technical assistance project. Indeed, UNCTAD and ASYCUDA aim at ensuring system and data ownership by the country, which can only be reached through intensive training. By limiting or removing intermediation, blockchain will directly contribute to reducing trade costs. Nevertheless, developing countries' exports rely heavily on intermediation to access foreign markets, which poses the question of the future role of intermediaries.

Source: UNCTAD.

Numerous companies and Governments are already forming consortia and alliances to deploy the blockchain technology in various areas of international trade. Several companies are also experimenting with the technology with their in-house technical teams. For instance, in 2018, the first blockchain-based Smart Bill of Lading was issued by CargoX for goods that departed from Shanghai to the Port of Koper, Slovenia,[7] at a little fraction of the usual cost of sending paper documents through courier services across the globe. The Global Shipping Business Network (GSBN)[8] has already started testing DLT to speed up efficiency in their work.[9] Tradelens,[10] the IBM and Maersk-led consortium of leading firms in the shipping and maritime industry, already leverages the technology in some areas of its ecosystem and has successfully trialled an electronic Bill of Lading on the platform(e-BL).[11] These efforts are fast ramping up with more shipping and maritime industry leaders taking the initiative to bring together competitors to collaborate for increasing efficiency.

[7] See https://www.marineinsight.com/shipping-news/first-ever-blockchain-based-cargox-smart-b-l-successfully-completed-its-historic-mission/.

[8] See https://www.cargosmart.ai/en/solutions/global-shipping-business-network/.

[9] See https://smartmaritimenetwork.com/2019/07/16/global-shipping-business-network-agreements-signed/.

[10] See https://www.tradelens.com/.

[11] See https://worldmaritimenews.com/archives/277649/cma-cgm-msc-to-become-members-of-tradelens-blockchain-platform/.

4. Value chains

As value chains grow more intricate, involving diverse stakeholders and relying on several external intermediaries, blockchain can be used to improve the transparency, traceability and reliability throughout the value chains by reducing information asymmetries, tracking inventories and ownership rights of products, enabling faster and more cost-efficient delivery of goods, and enhancing coordination between stakeholders (Gaur and Gaiha, 2020; Allen et al., 2018).

While blockchain-driven value chain use cases are still emerging, several successful proof-of-concept implementations suggest that blockchain will likely lead to disruptive transformations, ranging from cost-savings and increased efficiencies to new operational models (see box 4 for examples). Tracking goods through the production and delivery process to ensure quality and authenticity or automated compliance to freight and trade regulations exemplify just two promising blockchain applications in value chains.

For instance, in response to food contamination scandals worldwide, Walmart has teamed up with IBM in tackling food safety in the supply chain using blockchain technology. Using the IBM Hyperledger Fabric, a blockchain-based platform, Walmart has successfully completed two blockchain pilots: pork in China and mangoes in the Americas. With a farm-to-table approach, Walmart's blockchain solution has reduced time for tracking mango origins from seven days to 2.2 seconds and promoted greater transparency across Walmart's food supply chain (Kamath, 2018). Other large companies are also exploring blockchain use cases. For example, Coke One North America has started a project on Ethereum to facilitate the onboarding process for Coca-Cola bottling suppliers. By August 2020, 12 of the largest North American Coca-Cola bottlers were using the blockchain platform for internal supply chain management and the nodes are expected to expand to external suppliers (Haig, 2020).

Outside the food industry, a blockchain-enabled platform developed by Everledger, a technology company, recorded the provenance of over 2 million diamonds along the supply chain. With a unique digital identity for every diamond, the platform can track and confirm the source and location of each diamond, preventing possible fraud and counterfeit.[12]

Another promising area for blockchain solutions is provenance within the pharmaceutical industry. Counterfeit pharmaceuticals pose serious risks for customers and society. According to the World Health Organization, an estimated 10–30 per cent of medicines sold in developing economies are counterfeits and every year more than 120,000 people die in Africa as a result of fake anti-malarial drugs (WHO, 2017). Countries like Saudi Arabia are committed to exploring the role of blockchain technology in the sustainability and effectiveness of the pharmaceutical supply chain, addressing problems such as medication shortage, lack of coordination among health-care stakeholders, product wastage and lack of medication demand information.[13]

In summary, blockchain potentially reduces transactional complexity, information asymmetry and contractual incompleteness, value chain risks decrease due to traceability, transparency, and openness of transactions and agreement records (Schmidt and Wagner, 2019).

[12] See https://www.everledger.io/our-technologies/blockchain-and-more/.

[13] Contribution from the Government of Saudi Arabia available at https://unctad.org/system/files/non-official-document/CSTD_ 2020-21_c27_B_Saudi%20Arabia_en.pdf.

Box 4 Examples of applications of blockchain in supply chains

FAO is supporting innovations in the supply chain through cooperation with other stakeholders which focus on agriculture and livestock, fisheries, forestry, conservation and rural development. In collaboration with ITU, national partners and technical service providers, FAO conducted a pilot project on pigs (livestock) using blockchain to create a database for traceability in Jiwaka, Papua New Guinea. Pig farmers were registered, and their pigs were ear-tagged with radio frequency identification (FRID) enabled tags linked to a traceability database. Farmers participate by inputting data (breed type, feed type, geography, incidences of pig disease and remedy) into the system until the pigs are ready for sale. Potential buyers can visit the pig selling points with an application and scan the ear-tags to access and view the history before making decisions. The integration of the blockchain technology in traceability enhances the sustainability of the livestock traceability system and the development and maintenance of similar block-chain-derived products and services in future.[14]

The charcoal project in Côte d'Ivoire is another promising FAO pilot project. Charcoal remains one of the most important sources of fuel in sub-Saharan Africa, including Côte d'Ivoire. A look through the supply chain highlights the interlinkages with issues of energy, deforestation, employment and other socioeconomic and environmental challenges. The Alpha version of the legal and sustainable charcoal traceability blockchain application was already developed and tested. One of the key findings is that blockchain has the potential to help build traceability systems that are more transparent, efficient and reliable.[15]

The need for innovative recycling solutions that promote environmental sustainability has never been greater. In Austria, the project Plastic Supply Chain – an innovative approach to offset plastic – aims to investigate the impact of technological and supply chain innovations in the process of plastic bottle supply chains by the shift from a linear to a circular supply chain. The project investigates how a circular supply chain may reduce plastic bottle waste across the relevant processes, i.e. source, transport, storage, make, deliver, revalorization and return. In this project, blockchain technology enables plastic flow visibility and supply chain data quality as well as data security. This innovative approach allows evaluating the impact of the implementation of incentives to obtain higher collection rates, consequently higher recycling rates and increased visibility of the plastic work in process.[16]

Blockchain also can be deployed in support of the humanitarian supply chain. Humanitarian agencies have to manage complex supply chains over huge distances under highly demanding circumstances. In 2020, the Foreign, Commonwealth and Development Office (FCDO) of the United Kingdom in close coordination with the German company Datarella and other FCDO stakeholders launched a pilot looked to test whether the use of a private blockchain platform could provide immutable proof of supplies passing between actors in the humanitarian supply. The pilot ended with a robust proof of technology that had tracked a live shipment of goods in a controlled environment. The platform was under continuous development to enable scale as well as insight into the "last mile" of humanitarian supply chains using satellite-connected mesh networks to overcome connectivity problems in last-mile humanitarian aid delivery. [17]

Source: UNCTAD, based on contributions from the Governments of Austria and the United Kingdom, and from FAO, available at https://unctad.org/meeting/commission-science-and-technology-development-twenty-fourth-session.

[14] Contribution from FAO available at https://unctad.org/system/files/non-official-document/CSTD_2020-21_c11_B_FAO_en.pdf.

[15] Ibid.

[16] Contribution from the Government of Austria available at https://unctad.org/system/files/non-official-document/CSTD_2020-21_c01_HB_Austria_en.pdf.

[17] Contribution from the Government of the United Kingdom available at https://unctad.org/system/files/non-official-document/CSTD_2020-21_c34_B_UK_en.pdf.

III. BLOCKCHAIN'S ECOSYSTEMS OF INNOVATION

Innovation in the blockchain technology is the process of bringing blockchain-based products and services to the market. As discussed in the previous chapters, blockchain is associated with a broad range of innovations, from specific products such as Bitcoin to platforms for the development of decentralized applications such as Ethereum. The ecosystem of innovation related to blockchain technologies sets the rate and direction of innovation and competence building on the blockchain technology. The central elements in the ecosystems of innovation are the main actors in the innovation process, their interlinkages through which knowledge and resources flow to enable innovation, and the institutions in place that set the rules, regulations and expected behaviour associated with blockchain innovation.

A. TYPES OF INNOVATION

There are different kinds of innovation related to blockchain. Each one of them involves different actors and interlinkages in the innovation ecosystem. In a first approximation, these innovations can be divided into cryptographic innovations, software infrastructure (layer 1) and application (layer 2), hardware infrastructure, governance and business models (meta-layer), and regulations.

1. Cryptographic innovations

At the most basic level, there are innovations related to the cryptographic elements of blockchain, including the algorithm, blockchain, mathematical models, etc. These innovations seek to address issues such as increasing security of the solutions, setting different levels of privacy and confidentiality, or address performance issues. Many of these innovations are buried behind obscure and complex concepts and are only comprehensible to a small set of developers with the required cryptographic skills and expertise. These innovations, many times, have the objective to address flaws that were discovered in previous implementations. The look and feel of the solution, the way that users interact with it, and the use case may not change with this kind of innovation. They can be classified within process innovations. Other times, these innovations in the cryptographic aspects of solutions open new possibilities to address new use cases, generating product innovations.

2. Layer 1 software infrastructure

Another kind of innovation is related to creating a basic software infrastructure (layer 1) on top of which blockchain application can be developed. Layer 1 infrastructure broadens the pool of developers by reducing the required crypto skills to program in that layer, and also reduces the risk of faulty crypto implementations. Platforms such as Ethereum and Flow provide a development environment of upper-layer applications that benefit from what is considered a reliable cryptoalgorithm and protocol infrastructure (see box 5 for a discussion on the

Box 5
Innovation in Ethereum

Since Ethereum was launched, its development and research have been in continuous progress. By October 2020, Ethereum was developing and planning to implement a series of upgrades clustered by the term Ethereum 2.0 (Eth2) improving the scalability and security of Ethereum protocol. A central element in this process is the splitting of the Ethereum network into smaller portions called shard chains. The Eth2, also known as Serenity, is designed to be launched in three phases:

Phase 0: The so-called beacon chain will be a new blockchain at the core of Ethereum that will provide consensus to all the shard chains. On every shard chain, miners will create blocks of transactions and report them to the beacon chain. This information will then become available to all the other shards – maintaining consensus across the whole network. At this stage, the consensus mechanism will transition from proof-of-work to proof-of-stake. Ethereum initial use the proof-of-work protocol relies on miners to keep the network secure by devoting a great amount of computing power to creating new blocks. Instead, the proof-of-stake mechanism keeps the network secure but replaces energy consumption with a financial commitment. The beacon chain is expected to be created in 2020; it was still under the testing phase in September 2020.

Phase 1: The shard chains will be created to take on a portion of the processing workload (transactions and account data) of Ethereum. Currently, all nodes in the Ethereum network must download, compute, store and read every transaction in the history of Ethereum before processing a new one, which constraints significantly the speed of executing transactions (15 transactions per second), which is 100 times slower than Visa's processing speed, around 1,500 transactions per second. These updates are expected to be implemented in 2021.

Phase 2: fully formed shards should be fully functional chains, compatible with smart contracts, and they will be able to communicate with each other more freely. Developers may be able to design shards in their own ways. This phase is in the research phase and, according to the plan, it will take place from 2021 onwards.

Source: UNCTAD, based on Ethereum 2.0 (Eth2) (2020).

innovation in Ethereum). Moreover, these platforms also provide ways for the implementation of interoperability between application in the platform, which tremendously increases the value of using the infrastructure. Many innovations in layer 1 infrastructure are related to the performance of the protocol.

3. Layer 2 software infrastructure

Perhaps the most visible face of the innovation ecosystem is the set of innovations related to the decentralized applications (layer 2). These can run on top of layer 1 infrastructure such as Ethereum or be implemented from scratch. Many of these innovations tend to focus on use cases that are a decentralized version of an existing centralized application or system – for example, decentralized currency exchange or trading platform. There are numerous use cases that have been mainly based on the premise that decentralization is indisputably better than centralization, without any further regard about the real value added in creating a decentralized version of an existing and, many times very successful, solution. Many of these decentralized applications have a look and feel of existing centralized applications.

4. Hardware

Innovations layer 1 and 2 have also driven innovations in the hardware infrastructure to support these applications. For example, the innovation in computers for mining cryptocurrencies – from the use of graphic cards to the development of specialized computers, there is a considerable level of innovation in the hardware area of blockchain to strike an economically optimum balance between increasing computer power for boosting the rate of cryptographic operations leading to successful mining and higher profits, while trying to reduce costs through reducing power consumption, maintenance, and replacement costs. With the increasing adoption of cryptocurrencies, one should also expect innovations related to gadgets such as smartphones and smartwatches as well as specific hardware for safely storing these cryptocurrencies.

5. Governance and business models

Another area of innovation in blockchain is related to the governance mechanisms and business models of blockchain solutions. Not only the use of the application can become decentralized with blockchain, but also the gains from the use of the solution, its development and even the governance of its development. One innovation that has emerged in this front is the concept of governance tokens that give their holders the ability to propose and vote on the changes that would be implemented in the solution. A related innovation is the DAO (Decentralized Autonomous Organization), which creates the possibility of a completely market-based organization, which has no employers and employees whatsoever, but that relies on a decentralized governance mechanism to function as an organization.

6. Innovations in regulations

The current time is the installation period of blockchain technology, and its innovations are in constant flux. This is a period in which there are more ideas and early implementations than the number of relevant use cases. However, due to the novelty around the technology and its applications, one only finds out if the use case is indeed relevant or not after some resources are committed in the initial implementation. Mistakes are made and, hopefully, corrective actions are taken. Therefore, in addition to technological corrections, many adjustments are needed in terms of institutions and regulations. This is another area of innovation (social innovation) that was brought about by technology. These innovations tend to trail the technological development and the innovators in this area are also learning what works or not.

B. ECOSYSTEM OF INNOVATION

According to the UNCTAD *Technology and Innovation Report 2021*, China and the United States of America lead blockchain research. During the period of 1996–2018, there were 3,390 publications related to blockchain led by the United States (670), China (622) and the United Kingdom (239). The top three affiliations were Chinese Academy of Sciences (61/China), Beijing University of Posts and Telecommunications (43/China) and Beihang University (31/China). During the same period, there were 2,975 patents, with the top three assignees' nationality being the United States (1,277), Antigua and Barbuda (300) and China (270). The current top owners were nChain (336/United Kingdom), Mastercard (181/United States) and IBM (134/United States).

Companies from the United States are the leading blockchain service providers. Top providers of blockchain (blockchain-as-a-service providers)[18] service include

[18] Blockchain-as-a-Service (BaaS) is when an external service provider sets up all the necessary blockchain technology and infrastructure for a customer for a fee. By paying for BaaS, a client pays the BaaS provider to set up and maintain blockchain connected nodes on their behalf. A BaaS provider handles the complex back-end for the client and their business.

Alibaba (China), Amazon, IBM, Microsoft, Oracle and SAP (Germany) (Akilo, 2018; Patrizio, 2018; Anwar, 2019). Top users of blockchain measured by spending on blockchain service were finance, manufacturing and retail sectors (IDC, 2019).

Despite the lead of the United States and China, the blockchain ecosystem of innovation is more global than for other frontier technologies such as AI. Innovations in blockchain have drawn on programmers from developed and developing countries, currency exchanges in several markets, mining distributed across the world – in places with cheap energy resources – and on a user base of retail traders and financial institutions from all over the world. The fact that innovation in blockchain has been directed mainly to financial and payment solutions, and that the financial sector is very global in nature, further contributes to the globalization of the ecosystem of innovation.

From Governments to enterprises, from research institutions to start-ups, the blockchain innovation ecosystem is constantly growing with stakeholders taking initiatives to foster blockchain's innovation. Most initiatives actively involve multiple actors from public research, industry and Government, have mixed public–private funding models and seek international cooperation on the blockchain. box 6 showcases some of the initiatives, both from the public and private sector, extracted by the contributions received from the Governments of the member States.

Many of the blockchain initiatives are based on open-source, free and readily available software for the global common good with not-for-profit principles at its core. Many of them are funded by not-for-profit foundations, many of which are registered in Switzerland. Examples are the Bitcoin Foundation, Ethereum Foundation, the Libra Foundation (founded by Facebook) and the Blockchain Charity Foundation (founded by Binance).[19] These are well-funded foundations that are to see to the success of their respective open-source software ecosystems or support other charity works.

Multinational companies operating in traditional sectors have also entered the space with different initiatives, such as Nestlé (track and trace) and BMW and Maersk (value chain management). By the nature of blockchain solutions, related to their global operations, these companies also contributed to making the innovation and deployment of blockchain applications more global.

New NGOs and research institutes specializing in blockchain technology are being established; an example is the Blockchain Research Institute,[20] an independent, global think tank funded by international corporations and government agencies. This could become a leading trend in the integration of the technology in NGO works and bring efficiency in the non-profit sector. The Porino Foundation, a non-profit based in Switzerland, for instance, through their Sustainability Chain Project[21] deploys blockchain-based applications for organizations working to advance the Sustainable Development Goals.

In academia, an increasing number of universities have designed courses specifically for the study of blockchain technology. Examples are the University of Nicosia, Oxford University, MIT and Cambridge University. In these courses, various aspects of the technology, ranging from programming to cryptoeconomics and blockchain strategy, are taught to industry experts and corporate leaders. Several blockchain companies are also collaborating with academic institutions on research and development, as well as product design. It is expected that at full maturity of the technology, a whole new ecosystem will emerge with academics, advisors, programmers, financial analysts and cryptoeconomists at its core.

[19] The Blockchain Charity Foundation—through its Blockchain Impact Fund—for instance has partnered with UNDP for social good in developing countries, initially donating US$1 million in 2018. See https://blokt.com/news/binances-blockchain-charity-foundation-partners-with-united-nations-development-program-to-use-blockchain-for-social-good.

[20] See https://www.blockchainresearchinstitute.org/.

[21] See https://sustainability-chain.com/.

Box 6
Examples of the ecosystems of blockchain innovation

Austria: The Government of Austria encourages interdisciplinarity in blockchain research and development. The Austrian Federal Ministry of Climate Action, Environment, Energy, Mobility, Innovation and Technology and the Federal Ministry of Digital and Economic Affairs jointly funded the Austrian Blockchain Center, an interdisciplinary research excellence centre with the mission to be the one-stop-shop Austrian Research Centre for Blockchain (and related) technologies to be applied in industrial applications such as Industry 4.0/IoT as well as financial, energy, logistics, Government and administrative applications. The interdisciplinary Research Institute for Cryptoeconomics at the Vienna University of Economics and Business was founded in January 2018 and is member of the Austrian Blockchain Center. This research institute aims to coordinate all blockchain and Web3 related research activities in a multifaceted and interdisciplinary way and to build a competence centre that connects researchers with practitioners.[22]

Belgium: Blockchain Innovation Center, inaugurated by Fujitsu in 2018 in Belgium, is created under the mission to revolutionize the way consumers and enterprises buy, sell and exchange goods and services and for organizations to transform their commercial and operational models. One area of expertise that the institution plans to develop is the use of blockchain for the design and implementation of Smart City services focusing on important aspects of the city of the future, such as sociological and demographic factors, societal organization, economic functioning and ecological challenges.[23]

Finland: The blockchain ecosystem of Finland is booming. On 25 May 2018, Helsinki hosted the Blockchain and Bitcoin Conference – the first conference in Finland that is a part of the international series Blockchain and Bitcoin Conference. The event was dedicated to the cryptocurrency trading and investments, the introduction of distributed ledger technology in business, the development of blockchain-based solutions, as well as the global issues of the technology's influence over society.[24] Helsinki also has a Bitcoin Embassy, a non-commercial organization and a platform for Bitcoin initiatives aimed at promoting cryptocurrency among citizens. On a monthly basis, it organizes meetings for cryptocommunity participants, including top Bitcoin holders and entrepreneurs.[25]

Portugal: An initiative in Portugal named Bee2WasteCrypto, involved multiple actors in making joint efforts to blockchain innovation and research for the management of waste. Bee2WasteCrypto is a project involving a company (Compta), two higher-education schools (Instituto Superior Técnico, NOVA Information Management School), and some of these schools' research centres. Over the summer of 2020, 12 master and undergraduate students developed new blockchain-based solutions for Regional Waste Management Utilities (RWMU) and behavioural change on the management of waste.[26]

Russian Federation: The ecosystem of blockchain projects of the Russian Federation is formed by three main groups of players: first, large State institutions of innovative development, such as the Russian Venture Company and its subsidiaries, especially those involved in the National Technological Initiative; second, the Skolkovo Foundation, a scientific and technological centre for the development and commercialization of advanced technologies in the Russian Federation; and, third, major banks including Sberbank, VEB.RF, Alfa-Bank and VTB and corporations such as Rostekh, Gazprom, Rosseti and Russian Railways.[27]

Turkey: The blockchain innovation environment in Turkey is also very dynamic and collaborative. A platform called Blockchain Turkey was founded in June 2018 by Turkey Informatics Foundation (TBV) and had reached 71 members from more than 10 different industrial sectors as of September 2020. The platform is operating to increase the national potential and public awareness of blockchain technology, to use its valuable benefits and to determine strategic priorities for the ecosystem by providing training, organizing events, producing and publishing relevant content, evaluating the current opportunities and application of blockchain technology.[28]

Source: UNCTAD, based on contributions from the Governments of Austria, Belgium, Portugal, the Russian Federation and Turkey, available at https://unctad.org/meeting/commission-science-and-technology-development-twenty-fourth-session.

[22] Contribution from the Government of Austria available at https://unctad.org/system/files/non-official-document/CSTD_2020-21_c01_HB_Austria_en.pdf.

[23] Contribution from the Government of Belgium and from: https://www.fujitsu.com/be/microsite/nblockchain/blockchain-innovation-center/

[24] https://finland.bc.events/

[25] https://finland.bc.events/article/digital-modernization-how-finland-builds-blockchain-ecosystem-87686

[26] Contribution from the Government of Portugal available at https://unctad.org/system/files/non-official-document/CSTD_2020-21_c23_B_Portugal_en.pdf.

[27] Contribution from the Government of the Russian Federation available at https://unctad.org/system/files/non-official-document/CSTD_2020-21_c25_B_Russia_en.pdf.

[28] Contribution from the Government of Turkey available at https://unctad.org/system/files/non-official-document/CSTD_2020-21_c33_B_Turkey_en.pdf.

C. FINANCING BLOCKCHAIN INNOVATION

A particularity in the blockchain ecosystem is the strong use of crowdfunding to finance innovations. As defined by Schumpeter (1939), “capitalism is that form of private property economy in which innovations are carried out by means of borrowed money.” In the case of the blockchain ecosystem, innovators are borrowing money from the users of the innovation. Initial Coin Offering (ICOs), as seen mainly in the 2017 bitcoin boom, and other innovative forms of distributed finance allow for fast ways to raise money for blockchain innovation (and for developing bubbles), setting this type of innovation apart from innovation in other technologies that tend to rely more heavily on traditional sources of finance (e.g. venture capital).

ICOs were promoted as an equivalent, in the blockchain ecosystem, of the traditional IPOs. Through ICOs, the original team of developers were selling tokens to finance the development of the solution. Those tokens would be required to use the application; thus, there was an incentive for potential users to acquire the tokens. Usually, a share of the tokens was distributed to the development team and initial investors. Some ICOs were able to raise an enormous amount of funds. The increased valuation of the tokens of the most sought-after solutions made some of the original development team and venture capitalist very wealthy. After the bust of 2017, ICOs were scrutinized by regulators in the United States. Some of the ICOs were considered to breach securities regulations, and their development teams had to pay high fees.

More recently, other forms of decentralized finance have emerged. Some have tapped into the high gains in the value of cryptocurrencies such as bitcoin to use them to finance the development of new solutions. Thus, the original innovators and investors in previous innovations become the new investors in the new innovations. Many of these innovations have implemented decentralized governance mechanisms, as discussed in previous chapters, and, thus, these new investors also become owners and potential innovators of the new solutions.

IV. THE POTENTIAL IMPACT OF BLOCKCHAIN ON THE ACHIEVEMENT OF THE SUSTAINABLE DEVELOPMENT GOALS

This chapter discusses how blockchain could impact the Sustainable Development Goals. The discussion focuses on how current visions that society attributes to blockchain could play out and what could be their impact on sustainable development. An interesting prior example is the Internet. An initial meaning that society placed in Internet technology was that it would create a "global village" that would spread equity, justice, and democracy. These were expectations based on technical characteristics of the Internet (cheap, instantaneous, two-way communication). These expectations did not realize, and the actual use of the Internet has a direct impact on sustainable development (positive and negative). In fact, similar hopes were raised by the telegraph, railways, then the telephone. One prediction about radical innovation may be that some of its most important effects in the long term will be felt in areas where it was hardly expected to matter at the beginning (for example, the impact of internal combustion engine on urbanism). Similarly, blockchain technology is in its infancy, and there many different visions of how the technology is likely to develop, which products will result from this development and the potential consequences of their use.

This chapter is divided into the analysis of forward-looking scenarios and unintended consequences. In terms of scenarios, it discusses existing visions of the technology, from the more modest to the more revolutionary. The chapter discusses what would take for a particular vision to materialize within the time frame of the Sustainable Development Goals (by 2030), where the greatest challenges for society lie, and who might be affected.

It is important to note that all these visions are conditional to technological changes, but more importantly, to changes in organizational and social habits, the economy, social and (in some cases) political institutions. Therefore, the discussion of the visions of blockchain does not imply an agreement with these visions, or that they are correct. It only means that these are some of the ways that society (or parts of the society) see the blockchain and its future impact. What this chapter tries to assess are these visions. What would need to happen for them to materialize, who will benefit, what is the potential impact in the environment, what are the societal challenges, what are the changes required in the current institutions, etc.

A. EXAMPLES OF BLOCKCHAIN APPLICATIONS THAT CONTRIBUTE TO THE SUSTAINABLE DEVELOPMENT GOALS

As with any technology, blockchain can be applied in solutions that contribute to the achievement of the Sustainable Development Goals. There are several examples of such applications, both in the context of developed and developing countries. Table 1 presents examples of blockchain-based solutions that contribute to each of the 17 Sustainable Development Goals. Many of these examples are still in the pilot phase or have been deployed, but no assessment of actual impact is available.

Table 1
Examples of blockchain applications that contribute to the Sustainable Development Goals

Goal	Example
Sustainable Development Goal 1: No poverty (1.4 Equal rights to ownership, basic services, technology and economic resources)	Digital identity against poverty In many countries, the poor do not have birth certificates or official identity documentation, thus cannot have access to government services and subsidies. In Thailand in 2019, the Electronic Transactions Development Agency (ETDA) of the Ministry of Digital Economy and Society embarked on the Digital ID Project to develop a nationwide digital identification platform aiming to use blockchain-based timestamping to authenticate and verify the digital identities of Thai citizens.[29]
Sustainable Development Goal 2: Zero hunger (2.1 End hunger and ensure access by all people, in particular, the poor and people in vulnerable situations)	Food voucher transfers with blockchain Blocks for Transport is a supply chain digitization initiative launched by WFP to increase the efficiency of the food transport between the Port of Djibouti through the Ethiopian supply chain corridor to destination warehouses. This initiative aims to deploy a private blockchain between the supply chain participants from whom authorization is needed. Building Blocks is another voucher delivery platform created by WFP to simplify voucher transactions by removing the need to create virtual custodial accounts with financial services providers. It is a large-scale deployment of blockchain and serves approximately 700,000 beneficiaries in two countries in 2020.[30]
Sustainable Development Goal 3: Good health and well-being (3.8 Access to quality essential health-care services)	A modernized information-sharing mechanism in healthcare The health-care system of Cuba is working in collaboration with the Electronic Technology Software Production Company (SOFTEL) for the management and exchange of medical information between different institutions in the country using blockchain technology. In 2019, with the support of SOFTEL, the hospital Manuel Fajardo implemented digital medical records that save the results of laboratories, CT scans, x-rays and other tests performed to patients. This data will be available to any health entity in the country once a centralized medical history is created at the national level.[31]
Sustainable Development Goal 4: Quality education (4.4 Increase the number of people with relevant skills for financial success)	Receive and share official credentials securely and efficiently Blockcerts is an open standard for issuing, viewing and verifying blockchain-based credentials for academic and professional certifications, workforce development and civic records. These digital records are registered on a blockchain, cryptographically signed, tamper-proof and shareable. The Goal is to enable a wave of innovation that gives individuals the capacity to possess and share their own official records. The initial design was based on prototypes developed at the MIT Media Lab and by Learning Machine, now Hyland Credentials. For ongoing development, this open-source project actively encourages other collaborators to get involved (Blockcerts, 2020).
Sustainable Development Goal 5: Gender equality (5.1 End discrimination against all women and girls)	Financial independence for women's empowerment VipiCash, a winner at the first "blockchain hackathon" coorganized by UN-Women and Innovation Norway in 2017, is an application that uses blockchain technology to enable secure money transfer among women so that they can have access and control over their own money, independent of the male members of their family. The founder, a social innovator who grew up in a refugee camp, is working to create blockchain solutions to help empower women in humanitarian crisis situations (UN-Women, 2018).
Sustainable Development Goal 6: Water and sanitation for all (6.4 Increase water use efficiency and ensure fresh water supplies)	Transparent and reliable water trading system In Australia, Arup, a multinational firm, is working with the government of the State of New South Wales to build a proof-of-concept that uses blockchain technology to improve the water trading system, so it is fairer, as well as more reliable, transparent and efficient to manage (Arup, 2018).

[29] Contribution from the Government of Thailand available at https://unctad.org/system/files/non-official-document/CSTD_2020-21_c30_B_Thailand_en.pdf.

[30] Contribution from WFP available at https://unctad.org/system/files/non-official-document/CSTD_2020-21_c41_B_WFP_en.pdf.

[31] Contribution from the Government of Cuba available at https://unctad.org/system/files/non-official-document/CSTD_2020-21_c04_HB_Cuba_es.pdf.

Sustainable Development Goal	Blockchain application
Sustainable Development Goal 7: Affordable and clean energy (7.3 Double the improvement in energy efficiency)	Blockchain-based solution for energy efficiency improvement In the Russian Federation, the power company Rosseti together with Waves Enterprise and Alfa-Bank have implemented a pilot project called "Energy Accounting Using Blockchain Technology" to increase energy efficiency through blockchain use for electric power metering. The project ensures transparency of the system of interactions and data exchange between electricity companies, as well as consumers of electricity.[32]
Sustainable Development Goal 8: Decent Work and Economic Growth (8.10 Universal access to banking, insurance and financial services)	Access to interest-free loans using blockchain In April 2020, the Federal Tax Service (FTS) of the Russian Federation launched a blockchain platform named "MasterChain" to issue interest-free loans to SMEs. The platform has been designed to rapidly process business owners' applications for interest-free loans fo the payment of wages. It transfers digital values and information about them between participants and includes several services.[33]
Sustainable Development Goal 9: Industry, innovation and infrastructure (9.1: Develop sustainable, resilient and inclusive infrastructure)	Blockchain-based cash register Latvia encourages e-government in all domains of Government and has also explored the use of blockchain systems in the public sector and government-provided services. A pilot project in Latvia involves the implementation of the cash register reform that would strengthen the supervisory capacity of the State Revenue Service (VID) by reducing unregistered cash flow and provide a proportionate financial and administrative burden for businesses to ensure compliance with the requirements set for them, thus reducing shadow economy. Blockchain-based cash register solution is also expected to ensure environmental sustainability by reducing paper use.[34]
Sustainable Development Goal 10: Reduced inequalities (10.3 Ensure equal opportunity)	Improve schools' Internet connectivity around the world The UNICEF Project Connect is a blockchain-based platform that aims to map every school in the world and their connectivity to help people understand what regions are lacking basic connectivity, then eliminate the digital divide, increasing opportunity for every community. The Goal is to provide real-time data assessing the quality of each school's Internet connectivity, eventually creating an observable metric of society's progress towards enabling access to information and opportunity for every community.[35]
Sustainable Development Goal 11: Sustainable cities and communities (11.2 Affordable and sustainable transport systems)	Blockchain makes cities inclusive, safe, resilient and sustainable The State Railway of Thailand uses blockchain in the development of a dedicated communications system to increase the accuracy of its railway itinerary and to enhance the security of high-value parcels shipped through its logistics network. The projects of transportation and logistics ultimate goals are to deploy the blockchain technology to make cities inclusive, safe, resilient, and sustainable where opportunities are provided for all, with access to basic services transportation and all of that in a sustainable way.[36]
Sustainable Development Goal 12: Responsible consumption and production (12.2 Sustainable management and use of natural resources)	Blockchain-based seafood traceability and quality control Bitcliq, a technological SME, developed a blockchain-based e-marketplace for seafood trading. This platform, named Lota Digital, allows fishers to register and post a sale for fishes and seafood on the platform. It provides a quality control service in the auction process and controls the trade agreements between the buyer and the seller with the use of blockchain.[37]

[32] Contribution from the Government of the Russian Federation available at https://unctad.org/system/files/non-official-document/CSTD_2020-21_c25_B_Russia_en.pdf.

[33] Ibid.

[34] Contribution from the Government of Latvia available at https://unctad.org/system/files/non-official-document/CSTD_2020-21_c21_B_Latvia_en.pdf.

[35] https://www.projectconnect.world

[36] Contribution from the Government of Thailand available at https://unctad.org/system/files/non-official-document/CSTD_2020-21_c30_B_Thailand_en.pdf.

[37] Contribution from the Government of Portugal available at https://unctad.org/system/files/non-official-document/CSTD_2020-21_c23_B_Portugal_en.pdf.

Sustainable Development Goal 13: Climate action (13.3: Build knowledge and capacity to meet climate change)	Low carbon tea project in Kenya (GLI-TEA) The project activities include a feasibility study and pilot testing on blockchain technology for the Kenyan tea sector. The use of blockchain supports the traceability and transparency of both production and emissions of the tea value chain. While increasing the trust among consumers and retailers, tea promoted as a “carbon sink” could give growers potential access to carbon markets, bringing forward economic incentives for small-scale tea producers.[38]
Sustainable Development Goal 14: Below water (14.2 Protect and restore ecosystems)	Rewards for protecting biodiversity in Australia The Commonwealth Bank of Australia, in partnership with BioDiversity Solutions Australia, has developed a prototype platform to facilitate the protection of environmental ecosystems, while also creating an alternative source of income for landowners and rewarding them for preserving biodiversity on their land and marine resources.The platform enables the creation of tradeable digital tokens named BioTokens, representing biodiversity credits for the Biodiversity Offsets Scheme of the government of New South Wales, within an efficient blockchain-enabled marketplace (Commbank, 2019).
Sustainable Development Goal 15: Life on land (15.7 Eliminate poaching and trafficking of protected species)	Incentive wildlife conservation in Namibia Wildlife Credits is a wildlife conservation incentive payment scheme developed and piloted by Namibian community-based natural resource management (CBNRM) organizations. They offer conservancies direct payments for wildlife sightings on their territory and for maintaining habitat, mainly in the form of migration corridors. In locations where the rule of law is not upheld, and the banking infrastructure is poor, payments for ecosystem services (PES) schemes can corrupt, and the payments sometimes fail to reach the addressees. This solution tackles these issues (Oberhauser, 2019; Wildlife Credits, 2020).
Sustainable Development Goal 16: Peace, justice and strong institutions (16.9 Provide universal legal identity)	Transparency in transactions and immutability of asset registration The Bank of Thailand adopted blockchain technology to minimize interbank settlement fees, and 22 banks in Thailand have come together to formalize the Thailand Blockchain Community Initiative which will streamline letters of guarantee via a shared trade finance platform. Blockchain enables transparency in transactions and the immutability of asset registration. Transparency ensures that commerce and trade documents, as well as other relevant data, are accessible to the public and available for criticism for better strategy-making in corporations and Governments to optimize trade and ensure standardization.[39]
Sustainable Development Goal 17: Partnerships for the goals (17.3: Mobilize financial resources for developing countries)	Blockchain platform to coordinate and trace international aid United Kingdom Aid, in collaboration with the fintech startup Disberse, launched a pilot to test whether using blockchain could solve problems of transparency, speed, efficiency and mismanagement of aid funding across the financial supply chain. Financial flows from donors represent huge sums of money but form complex networks of dependencies that are hard to understand at each level. Such a traceability problem means that not enough is known about the complete system to be able to analyse its effectiveness. A blockchain-enabled platform is used to coordinate and trace international aid transactions using smart contracts, combined with a virtual money account that is linked to a registered banking provider. Together, this solution can improve the overall speed, cost, and transparency of funds across the financial supply chain.[40]

Source: UNCTAD, based on contributions from the Governments of Cuba, Thailand, the United Kingdom and from WFP, available at https://unctad.org/meeting/commission-science-and-technology-development-twenty-fourth-session.

[38] Contribution from FAO available at https://unctad.org/system/files/non-official-document/CSTD_2020-21_c11_B_FAO_en.pdf.

[39] Contribution from the Government of Thailand available at https://unctad.org/system/files/non-official-document/CSTD_2020-21_c30_B_Thailand_en.pdf.

[40] Contribution from the Government of the United Kingdom available at https://unctad.org/system/files/non-official-document/CSTD_2020-21_c34_B_UK_en.pdf.

B. FORWARD-LOOKING SCENARIOS

1. Decentralized applications overtake centralized ones

Some people see blockchain only as a tool for creating decentralized applications that could efficiently replace existing centralized ones (those based on centralized databases) or allow for the creation of new applications that require decentralization. This development could facilitate innovation for the Sustainable Development Goals if blockchain could create solutions that otherwise would not exist by not being technically, economically or socially feasible as a centralized application.

This vision of the technology and its use is the basic extrapolation of the most evident characteristic of the technology: its decentralized nature. However, it is important to note that blockchain is not the only way to create decentralized applications. In fact, decentralized use of solutions is a common feature of the applications on the Internet. They are used in platforms such as Facebook and Airbnb. These applications, despite the decentralized use, still require centralized control of the data, and this is what the blockchain technology can decentralize. But when is decentralization a relevant feature of the application? The question, indeed, boils down to when to use a central database or a decentralized ledger.

There are several heuristics proposed to guide the development of blockchain applications and select between a traditional database and a DLT (United Nations Innovation Network, 2019). In these guidelines, usually, the decision for central databases is the most straightforward one. They recognize that most of the applications could be implemented with centralized databases, and only when the risk of centralized solutions is considered too high by the users, is a blockchain solution proposed.

In the original use case of the technology, the bitcoin, this risk was the power of a central actor to shut down the whole system or change the ledger and move away with other people's money. Given the financial implications, the solution justified the use of a DLT. However, this case is weaker for a considerable number of applications that people seems to be comfortably using today. In fact, users of most social networks are willing to trade their right for data privacy in return for the benefits of being part of the network. As long as the application works, users tend to be indifferent (and in fact, totally unaware) of the underlying technology used to power the applications that they use.

Therefore, on the social side, it would require a shift in the perception of the potential risk of using centralized applications for the demand for these applications to truly grow organically. In the absence of that, the push for decentralized applications will have to continue to be supply-driven – by the developers and promoters of the technology. The consequence of that pattern is that it is less likely that blockchain innovation would incorporate the user's views in the development of applications, which could make these solutions less effective in addressing relevant problems and challenges faced by users.

The blockchain technology has also to improve on the performance front to match the current performance of centralized applications. At this moment, it is not clear if that would be achieved soon. Current applications in finance, online payment and management of value chains are usually based on use cases that focus on properties such as freedom from central control and transparency, not on performance in terms of the number of transactions per unit of time. Perhaps more concerning, the use of proof-of-work in the blockchain as the consensus mechanism is extremely energy inefficient, as discussed later in this chapter. The more applications that use the proof-of-work, the larger that problem will become, and the higher the probability that people will start to notice and reject to use a technology that puts the climate or the planet in danger. A clash between two strong calls by civil society may be seen: the environmental call for action to address climate change and the call for freedom from central controls in the digital world. The latter seems to have the upper hand, currently.

If indeed decentralized applications overtake the current landscape of centralized ones, what would be the impact on the Sustainable Development Goals? A first one was already mentioned above; if the current proof-of-work mechanism is the way that most of the applications use to reach consensus (as currently is the case), then a world using blockchain technology replacing centralized ones would have a severe negative impact of the environment, and thus the Sustainable Development Goals.

The positive impacts are less clear. There is an expectation of reduced costs of use of solutions that use blockchain, due to potential reduction on transaction costs. However, there is nothing in the technology that intrinsically requires transaction costs to be low. In fact, the so-called "gas"

in Ethereum platform, which could be considered as the tax that users must pay for miners to register their transactions in the blockchain, has reached incredibly higher levels in August and September 2020. At that time, some users were paying $11 per transaction in gas fees (Toti, 2020). In the end, it is not clear if blockchain applications would be systematically more affordable for users than the centralized ones that they may replace.

What about the claim that the technology may enable new decentralized solutions for the Sustainable Development Goals, that otherwise could not be implemented using centralized databases? This seems to be a weaker claim because arguably the roadblocks for implementing technological solutions for the Sustainable Development Goals are usually not in the technologies themselves but on the access to these technologies, including availability, affordability, awareness, accessibility and ability to use. The fact is that the people that would benefit the most, those that are furthest behind in the Sustainable Development Goals, are also those that have less access to technological solutions. Inequality in terms of benefiting from technology reflects the existing inequalities in society, and can further exacerbate them (UNCTAD, 2020). It is conceivable that blockchain could be used in Sustainable Development Goal applications for which alternative centralized solutions are not viable due to the lack of trust of potential users in the motives, effectiveness, and reliability of the central (or incumbent) operator. However, that may also reflect deeper inequalities in power relations which could be difficult to address based only on technological solutions.

If despite these weak prospects, blockchain technologies replace centralized ones in technology solutions for the Sustainable Development Goals, that would not trigger the need for much change in the institutions that are in place to promote the use of ICT for development. A push would still be required for universal access to the Internet and for the mobile devices that allow the use of the applications. Similarly, Governments should continue to push for increasing the digital skills of the population. Laws and regulations related to data privacy and security would continue to be critically required.

2. Applications are developed for financial inclusion

Some people see blockchain as a tool that would allow people to have access to financial services at low costs; banking those that are connected but are also un-banked. The idea is that the potential for reduction in transaction fees through the decentralized nature of the blockchain would allow the poor to have access to retail banking services. This could be, for example, creating blockchain versions of MPesa or digital microcredit services, but with lower fees. The argument is that by not requiring a central authority to control or enable the transactions, which would need to be remunerated for that service, there would be savings to be made for the users of blockchain-based financial applications. The use of blockchain would also make services like MPesa and microcredit services more secure in certain aspects and more private (decentralized nature of the blockchain). Therefore, as a tool for financial inclusion, applications using blockchain could complement the services provided by retail banks.

As countries look to implement the blockchain technology to advance financial inclusion, the prospects of digital currency versus cryptocurrencies must be evaluated. Digital money has brought financial services to millions of people who previously did not have access to traditional banking. The technology uses the ubiquity of mobile phones to bring easy and fast digital cash transactions to new users. Whereas traditional banking has high barriers to entry and limited services outside of urban areas, digital money only requires SIM cards and basic identification to register new users. Blockchain technology has also seen similarly fast adoption in places where traditional banking cannot meet the needs of users. There are relative advantages to each system, and there is scope for both technologies to operate in tandem.

Digital money such as MPesa in Kenya has the advantage of being cheap and easy to use, operated with accessible mobile apps and a distributed network of agents that manage the cash to digital money exchange. Currently, cryptocurrencies have a higher technological barrier to entry. Easily operable and user-friendly applications are yet not readily available. Cryptocurrencies also require higher digital literacy to operate than mobile banking, and consensus-based algorithms take longer to verify a transaction than mobile banking transfers. Currently, for everyday usage, mobile banking is easier to use than cryptocurrencies for domestic transactions.

The fast adoption of digital money is not a deterrent to the adoption and use of cryptocurrencies. Each system has its strengths and can be used complementarily to serve different needs. As cryptocurrencies become more user-friendly, and if they succeed in becoming less resource-intensive (e.g. computing power, energy), the current users of digital money may become the cryptousers of the near future.

However, it is important to note that cryptocurrencies that are more suitable for financial inclusion are those that maintain relative price stability, the so-called stable coins. If the price of the cryptocurrency is volatile, such as in the case of Bitcoin, it becomes less useful as a mean of exchange. Mobile money such as in the MPesa is usually pegged to the national fiat currency. To become an alternative to mobile money, cryptocurrencies should have similar mechanisms.

Interestingly, one of the initial visions for Bitcoin was to facilitate financial inclusion. However, its high volatility and deflationary tendency, in which the expectation of holders of Bitcoin is that it will increase in value over time in comparison with any basket of products, makes Bitcoin ill-suited for day-to-day low-value transactions, as it is further discussed later in section IV.B.4. In addition, its speculative appeal as a crypto version of gold (holder of value) has tilted the ownership of Bitcoin towards wealthy investors, in a pattern that is the opposite to what would be expected from a tool for financial inclusion. Given that Bitcoin is the most successful cryptocurrency, it remains to be seen the emergence of cryptocurrencies that could make substantial contributions to more inclusive finance.

The whole area of decentralized finance (DeFi) could also contribute to financial inclusion, with the creation of decentralized versions of microfinance and other inclusive financial mechanisms. Currently, as mentioned in previous chapter, DeFi is going through a period of fast innovation. Most DeFi applications are related to currency exchanges and yield farms – platforms that enable people to lend cryptocurrency in return for interests and fees. The users are, in their majority, people with an above-average understanding of blockchain and finance. Many are developers themselves or DeFi "experts". Therefore, DeFi innovation ecosystem is not targeting the development of applications for the unbanked. Inclusiveness is not one of the drivers of innovation in this domain.

For the vision of blockchain technology as a tool for financial inclusion to materialize, there must be a push for inclusive financial innovations. It is unlikely that the private sector will drive this process because it tends to focus first on solutions for wealthier users, who can pay the further development and deployment of the applications. Therefore, Governments, civil society organizations and international organizations would need to steer the incentives for innovation towards inclusive finance and away from financial innovations that focus on making profits out of speculation and the valorization of cryptoassets, in a casino economy.

If, through the efforts of governments and other stakeholders, the private sector develops blockchain innovations for financial inclusion, what would be the impact on the Sustainable Development Goals? As per the discussion above related to digital money and cryptocurrencies, the expectation could be that blockchain applications could complement other digital versions of inclusive financial applications. However, it is not clear how much it would add beyond what the latter already offer.

An exception is in the case of people in countries undergoing macroeconomic distress such as hyperinflation. In that case, the decentralized nature of some blockchain applications would make these a safer option for people to store and manage their money. This situation is also discussed below in section IV.B.4.

3. Efficiency increases in international digital transactions

Some people consider that blockchain's main role is for increasing efficiency in digital transactions internationally. It would complement or replace interbanking and digital payment mechanisms. It could reduce the costs of remittances and payment transactions in supply chains and increase e-commerce.

As they can be exchanged without banks, cryptocurrencies do not impose the same transaction fees as digital currencies when exchanged cross-nationally. Sending remittances through traditional channels can often be expensive. Remittance costs averaged 7 per cent globally in the first quarter of 2019, and costs can be as high as 10 per cent in many African and Pacific island countries.[41] Regulation and lack of competition are the usual culprits of high remittances fees. Often, these transaction costs are flat fees which burden low-income workers more. In these cases, digital money such as MPesa may not be an option, given that such money is usually valid only for exchange with the local fiat currency. If cryptocurrencies become better trusted through standardization and regulation, they may reduce both transaction time and costs for remittances and lead traditional channels to provide competitive prices.

Many firms in low- and lower-income developing countries do not engage in international trade due to the lack of "hard" currencies (such as United States dollars) to carry out international transactions, which is a result of the lack of a diversified economy and exportable products.

41 See https://www.worldbank.org/en/news/press-release/2019/04/08/record-high-remittances-sent-globally-in-2018.

In countries with balance of payments difficulties (e.g. drop in exports, high import dependency, declining capital inflows, rising foreign debt and sustained currency overvaluation), Governments are forced to control the purchase of foreign exchanges and prioritize some sectors considered of national interest. Firms in other sectors would not have the required foreign currency to buy imports (e.g. capital goods and intermediary goods) that may be required for them to engage in exports.

The use of payment applications using blockchain could provide an alternative to firms to circumvent these restrictions. However, at the end of the day, such application would only work against the goals of public policy; for example, to prioritize firms in some strategic sectors in the access to foreign currency to promote social goals, such as the creation of higher-wage jobs or economic diversification and structural transformation.

Firms would still need to exchange cryptocurrencies to the local fiat currency to be able to pay workers, suppliers, and taxes, but if there is a decentralized marketplace for the exchange of cryptocurrency and fiat currency, that exchange could be done. However, there is always the possibility of the government to regulate the use of cryptocurrencies and restrict the exchange to local fiat currencies.

If indeed blockchain is used for international payment and digital transactions, what would be the impact on the Sustainable Development Goals? Increasing trade and transport efficiency and reducing costs has the potential to increase trade. Who benefits from that increase still depends on many other factors such as the productive structure of countries and the policies in place to harness trade for development. If most people in a low-income developing country continues to live out of subsistence agriculture, few cash crops and low-wage low-technology manufacturing, then increasing trade does not change the structure of their economy, and any gain is likely to be passed to foreign clients as lower prices. The challenges for developing countries to fairly integrate into and benefit from globalization would remain in a future in which blockchain is the main technology used for international digital transactions. Therefore, the impact of blockchain on sustainable development under this scenario, should not be expected to be significant.

4. Cryptocurrency replaces fiat money

This is the vision that blockchain cryptocurrencies could complement or replace fiat currencies. Money has been in existence throughout history in different manifestations. It has three primary economic functions: medium of exchange, store of value, and unit of account (Jevons, 1876). How well cryptocurrencies could serve those three functions would determine cryptocurrencies' prospects for replacing fiat money.

One measure of the extent to which a currency is being used as a medium of exchange is the number of transactions performed in that currency. As noted above (see chapter I, section B.1), both in terms of performed transactions and the number of users, at present, cryptocurrencies are far from challenging the dominant usage of sovereign currencies and no Government accepts them as a legal tender. Another indicative measure of cryptocurrencies' worth as a medium of exchange is the acceptance of cryptocurrencies as a means of payment. Currently, there are a limited number of merchants worldwide (predominantly, but not exclusively, Internet-based vendors) that accept cryptocurrencies as a means of payment. Some examples are Microsoft, which accepts Bitcoin for use in its online Xbox Store since 2014; Overstock, an online shop with furniture and home appliances, which accepts not only Bitcoin but also multiple other altcoins; Whole Foods, an Amazon-owned food retailer; Expedia, an online travel booking agency; Newegg, an online shop with electronics; Shopify, an e-commerce platform; and Coincards, which is a platform that exchange cryptocurrencies for gift cards that can be spent at retailers such as Apple, Amazon, Adidas, Walmart and Uber (Tuwiner, 2020). Thus, some cryptocurrencies are serving as a medium of exchange, although their acceptance is currently limited.

Another property of money is the store of value. How good a fiat currency (such as cryptocurrency) is in storing value depends on the monetary policy associated with that currency. If too much of it is created (faster than the average productivity increase of sectors of the economy), the cryptocurrency will be inflationary. Over time, more of it will be required to buy the same basket of products. The cryptocurrency will fail in the criteria of a store of value. If, on the other hand, too little of the currency is created, as compared with the average productivity increase in the economy, then the cryptocurrency will be deflationary. Less of it will be needed overtime to purchase the same basket of products. The cryptocurrency will be a good store (and increase) of value, but people will prefer not to use it for day-to-day transactions as it will have much more value in the future. Therefore, the currency may fail in the criteria of being a good medium of exchange.

Taking Bitcoin as an illustrative example, it seems a very good store of value, but ill-suited as a medium of exchange. On 22 May 2010, the first real-world transaction was recorded in which Bitcoin served the function of a medium of exchange, at a rate of US$0.0025 by buying two pizzas in Florida (United States) for 10,000 BTC (CoinDesk, 2014). Those two pizzas cost the equivalent to over US$100,000,000 by the exchange rate between Bitcoin and the United States dollar in October 2020.

An asset's worth as a store of value rests on people's beliefs regarding its future supply and demand (Bank of England, 2014). In the case of cryptocurrencies, this is partly determined by the algorithm that implements the cryptocurrency in the blockchain and partly by the expectations that people have related to that currency. Taking Bitcoin again as an example, in the supply side, a new block in Bitcoin blockchain is created every 10 minutes. By solving the cryptographic puzzle associated with the creation of a new block, the miner is rewarded with newly issued Bitcoins – the amount of the reward halves every 210,000 blocks, or roughly every four years. For the first 210,000 blocks, the reward associated with each block was 50 bitcoins. Starting on 28 November 2012, after the first 210,000 blocks were mined, the reward was halved to 25 bitcoins; on 9 July 2016, after another 210,000 blocks were mined, the reward halved to 12.5 bitcoins per block; and once again, on 11 May 2020, the reward was halved to 6.25 bitcoins. The reward is programmed to halve until the incremental addition of coins disappears around the year 2140 peaking at the supply limit of 21 million Bitcoins.[43] Figure 4 shows the actual supply growth of Bitcoins and its growth rate. Actual numbers are shown for the years 2009–2020, while projections are used for all other years (Bank of England, 2014).

While the supply growth is fixed and predictable, prospects for future demand, which is essentially market-determined, are far less certain. As cryptocurrencies lack any intrinsic demand (for use in the production or consumption) and any form of central authority, an opinion about their future demand should largely rest on (a) a belief about their future use as media of exchange and (b) a belief that they will continue to remain in demand even further into the future (Bank of England, 2014). The market value of cryptocurrencies will rise sharply when their adoption increases, while large liquidations of holdings will cause the price to plummet.

Figure 4
Bitcoin: Money supply and inflation

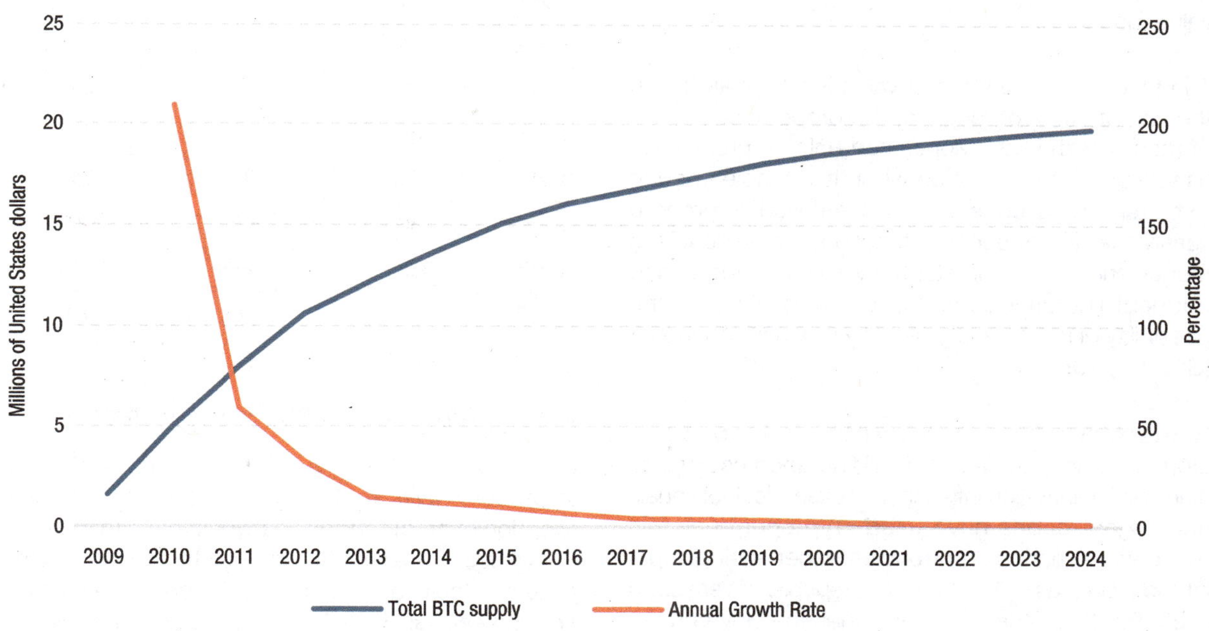

Source: UNCTAD, based on data retrieved from coinmetrics.[42]

[42] See https://coinmetrics.io.

[43] See https://bitcoin.org.

Figure 5
Price volatility of bitcoin

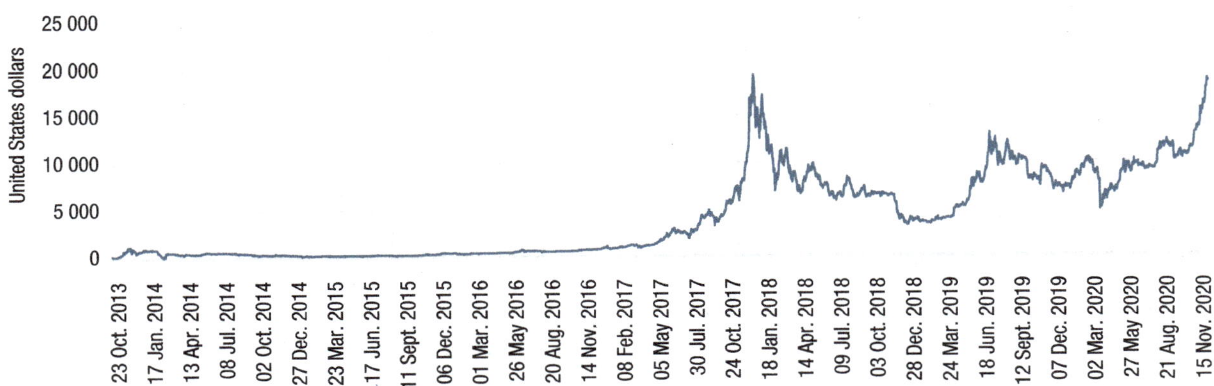

Source: UNCTAD, based on data from coinmarketcap.[44]

At present, all cryptocurrencies are characterized by unstable market values expressed in sovereign currencies (mostly in United States dollars). For example, figure 5 displays the historical price evolution of Bitcoin, and Table 2 shows the annual rate of return for Bitcoin in the period 2011–2019. Although these statistics drive interest in the analysis of cryptocurrencies as investments, they reveal the extremely volatile price and annual return that make Bitcoin unusable as a long-term unit of account for goods and services. Moreover, this value instability could also be considered the key factor of their failure to perform the store of value function.

The function of the store of value is interrelated with the unit of account function; the property of stability of money is the link. Money can only be predictably usable as a store of value when it is stable enough to be reliably saved, stored and retrieved. In order to satisfy the unit of account function, the value of the money should also be stable over time; sudden and frequent fluctuations of money value diminish the possibility of its usage significantly as a unit of account (Graham, 1940).

However, even if a cryptocurrency is only good as a store of value, people could still find good use of it as a hedge against high inflation. For example, individuals and organizations have used cryptocurrencies in response to national currencies experiencing rapid inflation, such as in the Bolivarian Republic of Venezuela in 2019.[45] In another example, when the Government of Argentina announced on 15 September 2020 a 35 per cent tax on purchases with cards (debit and credit) in foreign currency (mainly United States dollars), trading volume for the DAI-ARS pair (that is, people trading DAI for Argentine pesos) has increased substantially and reached record levels (BCRA, 2020; Jose and Lanz, 2020).[46]

Table 2
Rate of annual return of bitcoin

Year	*Opening price*	*Closing price*	*Annual return (Percentage)*
2011	0.3	4.72	1 473
2012	4.72	13.51	186
2013	13.51	758	5 511
2014	758	320	-58
2015	320	430	34
2016	430	968	125
2017	968	13 860	1 332
2018	13 860	3 742	-73
2019	3 742	7 193	92

Source: UNCTAD, based on data retrieved from coinmetrics.[47]

Thus, what is the viability of this vision of cryptocurrencies replacing fiat money? Firstly, the adoption of cryptocurrencies would have to increase many folds. For example, although the current market value of Bitcoin, as a representative cryptocurrency, is already very significant in absolute terms, it is lower at

[44] See https://coinmarketcap.com/currencies/bitcoin/.
[45] See https://www.rollcall.com/2019/09/10/venezuelans-use-cryptocurrency-to-bypass-corruption-inflation/.
[46] DAI is a stablecoin of the MakerDAO lending system. Available at https://makerdao.com/en/.
[47] See https://coinmetrics.io.

Figure 6
Comparison between Bitcoin and other assets on the global market

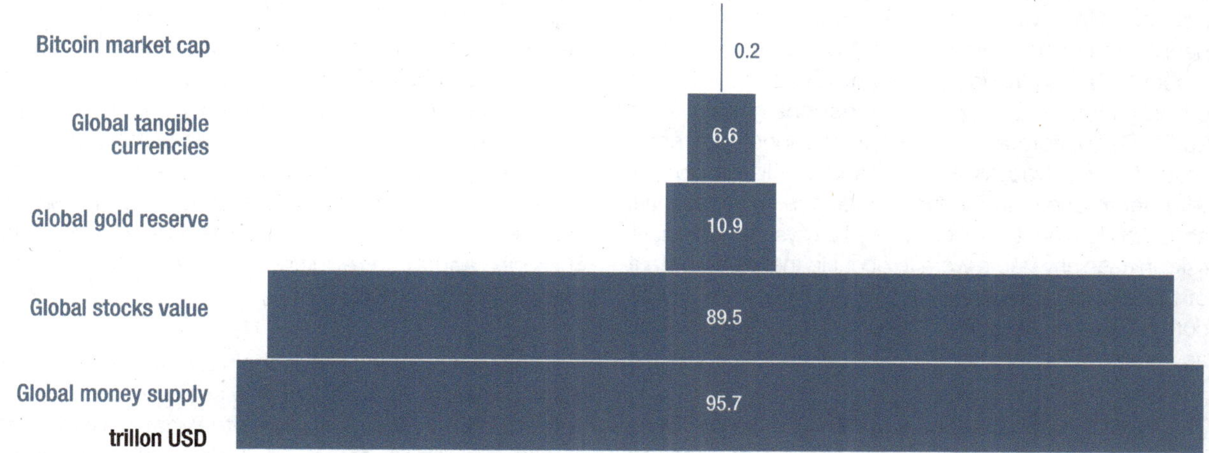

Source: UNCTAD, based on data from Desjardins (2020).

the aggregate level in comparison with other assets on the global market (figure 6). It represents 3.03 per cent of the world's total tangible currencies, namely, coins and banknotes in circulation (US$6.6 trillion), 1.83 per cent of world's gold reserve (US$10.9 trillion), 0.22 per cent of the world stocks value (US$89.5 trillion), 0.2 per cent of the global money supply (US$95.7 trillion) (Desjardins, 2020).

Moreover, the adoption of cryptocurrency as money for trade activities has not yet happened. Most Bitcoin buyers just hold on their bitcoins for speculative purposes. The fact that Bitcoin is not pegged to any currency exposes bitcoin holders to currency exchange risks. Stable coins do not offer a satisfactory alternative either because of the regulatory constraints to use them for trading and purchasing activities.

Based on these figures and examples, it could be concluded that, at the current stage of usage, cryptocurrencies have a negligible impact on the money supply and do not have the capacity to challenge the dominant position of sovereign currencies and central banks. Nevertheless, the influence of cryptocurrencies on sovereign currencies in the future cannot be predicted simply based on the current data because of fast progress in the area of information technologies, which hereafter might increase the chances for cryptocurrencies to compete with sovereign currencies effectively.

If cryptocurrencies indeed have a widespread adoption allowing them to replace fiat money, what would be the impact of that change for the Sustainable Development Goals? The impact would be felt through the effect on monetary policy. Cryptocurrencies represent a form of private money, that is, they are not issued and controlled by central banks, but rather by private entities.

The idea of coexistence of sovereign-backed and privately issued money is not recent. For example, in the 1970s, during a period of high inflation in western economies, the idea of free banking and private money was proposed by Friedrich Hayek. He was sceptical about a Government's monopoly on monetary policy and advocated abolishing the State's monopoly on issuing and regulating money and creating competitive supranational currencies as a way to ensure the stability of the official currency. He argued that it "… has certainly not helped to give us a better money than we would otherwise have had, and a very much worse one…" (Hayek, 1976).

However, any discretionary decisions made by private entities concerning the money supply could have an impact on the ability of central banks to conduct monetary policies such as the management of money supply and interest rates. Stablecoin with worldwide expansion expose small and economically weak States to a risk of substitution to their national currencies.

Several hurdles need to be lifted before regulators would consider authorizing a cryptocurrency to be used for economic transactions similar to those in a sovereign currency. One example is Libra, a project of Facebook for a global stable coin, backed by 28 major companies, among which are Visa, Master Card, Pay Pal and eBay, with a potential client base of 2 billion people (the users of Facebook). None of the Group of 7 countries authorized its use, and it has still not been officially launched despite its announcement in June 2019. Regulators asked Libra to demonstrate that it protects the privacy of its users and that it can comply with anti-money-laundering regulations. The potential abuse of dominant position, as well as systemic financial risks in case any failure were to occur in the management of Libra and or its reserves are also put forward as concerns to be addressed before authorizing Libra (or any stablecoin).

The momentum for a digital currency has now been initiated, and Central Banks have realized the need to develop their own digital currency should they want to avoid the private sector to get full control over digital currencies. China has been the first to initiate the race to Central Bank Digital Currency (CBDC). Pilot projects have started in some limited cities.

The European Central Bank (ECB) is also looking into launching its own digitized euro to complement the existing means of payment within the Eurozone but also to provide an alternative to private digital currencies.[48] Although DeFi has not been developed yet in CBDC, it took less than two years for its development on the Bitcoin and Ethereum platforms. It remains to be seen what the settings of the Chinese and European CBDCs will be, and who will be able to access these digital currencies and what will be the regulations to develop financial services and applications on these platforms.

5. Blockchain becomes the "new Internet"

This vision of blockchain considers that blockchain is a general-purpose technology (GPT) at the scale and scope comparable to the Internet. Blockchain would become the "Internet of value".

Some of those that subscribe to this vision consider that it automatizes trust, and thus can serve as a universal "trust machine". Blockchain technology would then revolutionize the way that firms operate (reducing transaction costs within the firm and enabling market solutions) and the way that markets function (creating markets that do not require a trusted third-party actor to design and enforce rules). However, others argue that with blockchain, trust is just shifted from one third party to another. For example, to use a cryptowallet, people must trust that the application works properly and does not have bugs or a malicious piece of code that will steal their cryptocurrencies. People also must trust the proper functioning of cryptoexchanges to be confident to use them. Similarly, people must trust the people that code blockchain applications and smart contracts. Such trust is ensured outside of a blockchain, through reputation, auditing of the code and smart contracts, and so on.

Another way to view Blockchain as the new Internet is to consider it is part of the set of technologies (others being AI, robots, IoT etc.) that is behind of the new sociotechnical revolution called Industry 4.0. The impact of such technological–economic revolutions goes beyond the economy; they change social relations, institutions, settlement patterns, the relationship with the environment and so on. These changes are truly transformative and affect the options open for countries to pursue sustainable development.

Based on that assumption, blockchain (as many of those frontier technologies listed above) is in the installation period of a sociotechnical revolution. The installation period is dominated by radical innovations led by suppliers, experimentation and new technological solutions, many standards and competing technical specifications. After the installation period, there is the deployment period in which the emphasis is on the exploitation of the technical solutions, changes in demand and lifestyles.

It is critical to understand the interrelation between the real economy and the financial sector throughout the life cycle of the technological–economic paradigm. During the installation period, the financial sector, which provides the required finance for entrepreneurs to carry out innovations, is also learning about the new technology and the opportunities that it creates for financial gains. This period is also usually characterized by considerable liquidity in the financial markets, due to high profits in the sectors associated to the previous technological–economic paradigm, which in the present is the Web 2.0 and the high profits of the main digital platforms (e.g. Facebook, Google etc.). The fast pace of innovation and insufficient knowledge about their real potential tends to create a frenzy of investment in the new technology. As a result, there is a tendency for speculation and the emergency of "money creating money" schemes with the

48 Christine Lagarde, President of the ECB at the opening session of the French–German parliament, 22 September 2020.

gradual decoupling of the real economy and the financial sector. The social–institutional basis of the economy (e.g. regulations, laws etc.) have not yet caught with the pace of innovations in the technolocial–economic sphere. There are no breaks for dealing with the casino economy driven by the financial sector. The end of the installation period is prone to financial bubbles and, thus, the installation and deployment period tend to be separated by financial crises. Such crises could lead to an alignment of institutions with the new technological–economic paradigm and recoupling of the financial sector with the real economy. The deployment period is then usually a "golden age" of innovations that percolate from the core sectors of the new technology to other sectors of the economy (Perez, 2002).

The way that blockchain innovation is self-financed could expedite this process and may create a series of periods of installation, crisis and deployment, particular to blockchain innovation. For example, one could say that from 2008 to 2017, there was a period of installation of blockchain technology focusing on cryptocurrencies (particularly bitcoin). There was a period of irruption and frenzy in relation to the technology (installation period), which fuelled the bitcoin bubble of 2017. The subsequent period, which has been called "crypto winter", has seen the involvement of other actors (including regulators) and a "normalization" of the development of cryptocurrencies, including with the interest of central banks. At the same time, the emergence of blockchain platforms such as Ethereum, smart contracts and the entire whole new set of innovations around DeFi could create the conditions for a new cycle of installation fuelled by self-financing mechanisms. The current rapid pace of innovation on DeFi could mark the new irruption phase, which could be followed by a new frenzy and a potential bubble on DeFi.

The fact that blockchain innovations include self-financing mechanisms allows for fast growth of financing the "next big thing" in the technology. The success of the early innovations fuels the search for additional ones in the same area, in this case, DeFi. Invariably, later case uses may become weaker and riskier, trying to stretch the technology and innovations to solve ever more obscure and less intuitive "problems". Speculation and search of fast gains attract investors that are less familiar with the real potential of the technology, which is a receipt for a frenzy. The potential recurrent boom and bust of blockchain innovations could bring changes in the regulations and other institutions needed to align finance and production capital (figure 7). However, that does not prevent the possibility that it could hurt many investors along the way.

If those affected are mainly the innovators and venture capitalists in the blockchain ecosystem, the boom-and-bust cycle may not create enough pain for potentially drastic, although required, changes in institutions. These cycles may be a curiosity in the eyes of outsiders. However, there is an increasing interest in the mainstream financial sector, and stories of small everyday investors who lost all their savings in the latest bust may start to be heard. Unfortunately, usually, only after many such cases, there is the required push for an institutional change of laws and regulations to address the risks.

Figure 7
Recurring phases in the blockchain innovation cycle

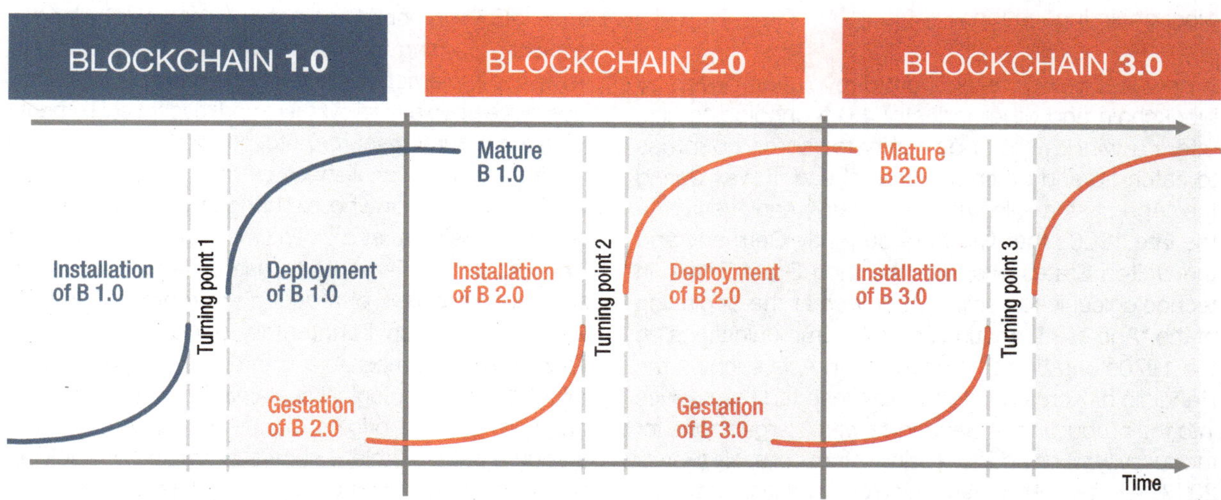

Source: UNCTAD, based on Perez (2002).

Awareness of the potential recurrent nature of this process is important for the understanding of the blockchain innovation. Given that all these innovations are being promoted under the same umbrella of blockchain technology, that may make it very confusing, particularly for those who are outside of the ecosystem, to understand at which stage the various innovations are. Innovations on the "new thing" will be in the irruption and frenzy phases, while the previous innovations will be a deployment period. Governments and their regulators, and civil society at large may be asking for, studying and proposing new regulations and laws that could address the previous boom and bust, but not a potential new one. Thus, it could create a situation in which regulators are constantly behind the curve, ever pressed to understand how to deal with the latest bust while the new one is already in the process of gestation.

Many of the innovations, as discussed in previous chapters, are global in nature. By focusing on the financial sector, they ride the long wave of the globalization of financial services that has been the reality of the past decades. New regulation and institutional change in such a globalized environment are extremely challenging. It would require a strengthening of international cooperation on finance and political will to tackle difficult problems, such as financial evasion.

Governments and regulators in developing countries usually face additional challenges due to low capacity and resources to keep abreast of the developments in the technology and the innovation ecosystem. There is an urgent need to support these Governments, particularly in low- and lower-income developing countries, including the least developed countries, in building their national capacities in engaging with blockchain innovation.

A new technological–economic revolution driven by blockchain and other Industry 4.0 technologies also offers a window of opportunity for some countries to catch up and others to forge ahead. It was during the "Age of steal, electricity and heavy engineering" in the late 1800s that what are currently Germany and the United States overtook the then Great Britain in technological leadership, and it was at the beginning of the "Age of information and telecommunications" in the 1970s and 80s that countries in Asia such as the Republic of Korea and Singapore inserted themselves into the production of electronics with a large scope for productivity gains and increasing returns of scale (Perez, 2002). A potential new technological revolution may offer the same opportunities for developing countries that are able to strategically diversify their economies into sectors that are associated with the new paradigm. Catching up would increase real incomes and government finances that could be used to accelerate the progress towards the Sustainable Development Goals.

C. POTENTIAL UNINTENDED CONSEQUENCES

This section discusses potential unintended consequences that require attention, regardless of the visions discussed in the previous chapters.

1. Environmental impact

High energy consumption presents one of the main issues of blockchain technology (particularly in its application to a bitcoin). The situation is changing as technology develops but, as the latest data show, due to the complicated validation and securing processes, bitcoin was using as much energy consumption as Switzerland (*BBC News*, 2019), and consumption has been growing in the recent years (table 3). This consumption generates CO_2 emissions that pose a threat to the environment. According to a recent study, the electricity used for Bitcoin produces about 22 megatons of CO_2 annually (Science Daily, 2020). That is as much as Kansas City in the United States. There is also considerable variation in the consumption of energy for the work of Bitcoin, that is, the result of the number of transactions in the blockchain. For example, the consumption of energy peaked first during the 2017 cryptocurrency boom (figure 8).

At the same time, the damage done by the energy use of one of blockchain's application – bitcoin – can be compensated by other blockchain possibilities (see box 7). Environmental and natural resource challenges are often coming from insecurity and the inability to verify the implementation of regulations and effectively incentivize people to follow them and respect entitlements to use a natural resource, etc. Blockchain could help to address these challenges by offering a secure and verifiable record of who exchanges what with whom and who has what at a given time. It also can be used to reinforce entitlements to use a natural resource, substantiate claims of reduced environmental impact and incentivize environmentally sustainable actions. There are several mechanisms through which blockchain might support ecological sustainability, but three main ones are product origins, behavioural incentives and resource rights. Table 4 shows examples of applying blockchain to environmental sustainability challenges in various sectors through these mechanisms.

Table 3
Environmental impact of Bitcoin

Electricity consumption by bitcoin	***Comparison***	***Year***	***Source***
67.4 tWh	Annual energy consumption of Switzerland	2020	Cambridge Bitcoin Electricity Consumption Center
45.8 tWh		2018	The Carbon Footprint of Bitcoin
22 tWh	Annual energy consumption Ireland	2015	Energy Market Barometer Report by GEM
Up to 215 kWh per transaction	Incandescent lightbulb of 25W burning for one year	2015	Energy Market Barometer Report by GEM
300 kWh per transaction reaching 900 kWh per transaction (by 2018)	More energy per transaction than all the world's banks put together	2018, 2019	Bitcoin Growing Energy Problem BBC news article

Source: UNCTAD.

Figure 8
Consumption of energy by Bitcoin
(TWh annualized)

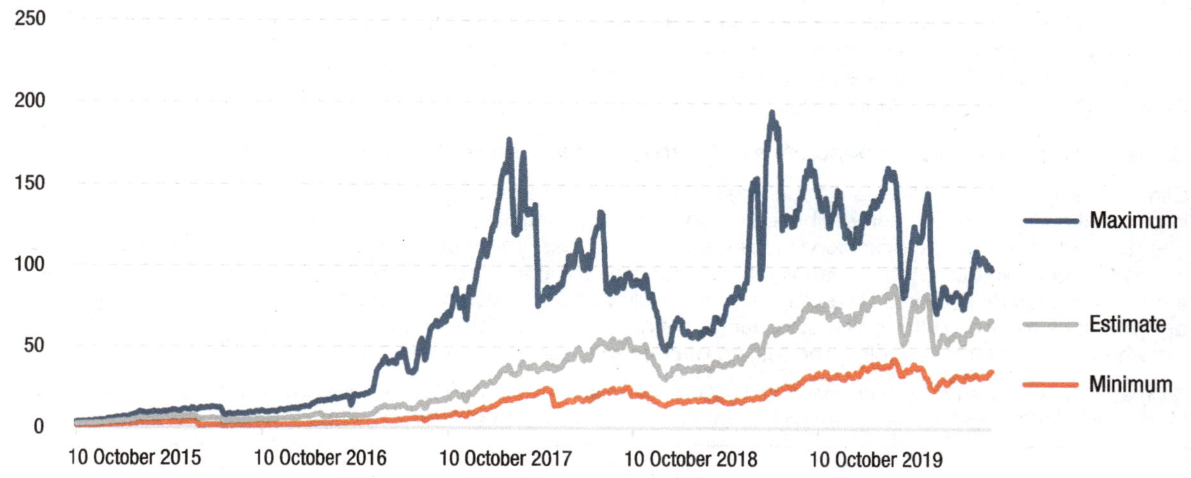

Source: UNCTAD, based on Cambridge Bitcoin Electricity Consumption Index.

Table 4
Mechanisms through which blockchain might support environmental sustainability

	Product origin	***Behavioural incentives***	***Resource rights***
Energy	Assurance about the environmental sustainability of production	Assurance about the reward for environmentally sustainable practices	Assurance about who has what right to what share of a natural resource
	Peer-to-peer trading in renewables		
		Renewables investment	
Forests	Sustainable supply chain traceability	Payment for ecosystem services	
Fisheries			
Water		Resource rights trading	

Source: Sève et al. (2018).

Box 7
Blockchain for climate change solutions

Blockchain can add value in the fight against climate change through contributing to greater stakeholder involvement, transparency and engagement and helping bring trust and other innovative solutions, leading to enhanced climate actions. Blockchain has been deployed to support climate-related projects in many innovative ways

Kultur-Token: a pilot project to incentivize climate-friendly mobility choices in Vienna

The development of the world's first Kultur-Token application (KT) was launched in Vienna in 2019. The KT is a governmentally owned application with the primary Goal of incentivizing citizens in Vienna towards sustainable mobility behaviours that reduce greenhouse gas emissions associated with cars. This pilot project rewards environmentally friendly behaviour with free admission to cultural events: in exchange for actively reducing CO_2 emissions by walking, cycling or using public transport, citizens receive a virtual token that they can exchange for tickets to renowned cultural institutions. The KT application uses motion tracking to measure the distances users travel in active travel modes and calculates their personal CO_2 balance (CO_2 saved by walking, cycling or using public transport compared to travelling the same distance by car).[49] The KT uses a Proof of Authority (PoA blockchain) technology, which is an adaptation of the Ethereum blockchain and is a less energy-intensive option than the traditional Proof of Work (PoW) technology.[50]

DAO IPCI: world's first transaction of green assets in the blockchain

The Russian Carbon Foundation initiated the development of the DAO IPCI platform in 2017 for green financial instruments (presented at the COP23, COP24 and COP25 climate conferences) and the Blockchain Climate Standard, a standard for issuance and verification of carbon units. DAO IPCI also develops smart contracts and blockchain technology-based independent ecosystems designed for carbon market instruments, including carbon compliance units, carbon-offset credits, environmental assets, accounting and transaction data. In 2020, based on the platform's experience, a new protocol was to be developed in partnership with the UNFCCC to issue and monitor green bonds using blockchain.[51]

Climate Ledger Initiative: a cooperative multi-stakeholder platform for climate change

Climate Ledger Initiative (CLI) is a Zurich-based platform that assesses and tests the potential of blockchain for implementing the Paris Agreement based on concrete applications in both developing and developed countries. The distributed nature of blockchain fits the decentralized, bottom-up structure of the Paris Agreement on climate change; it can help build and manage globally accepted solutions and enhance trust in international cooperation among multiple stakeholders. The CLI addresses policy and research questions and identifies specific innovation opportunities to contribute to climate change mitigation and adaptation and accelerate the implementation of the Paris Agreement by enabling the testing of concepts and approaches in concrete use cases.[52]

Source: UNCTAD, based on contributions from the Governments of Austria, the Russian Federation and Switzerland, available at https://unctad.org/meeting/commission-science-and-technology-development-twenty-fourth-session.

2. Criminal activities

Cryptocurrency may have a special appeal for criminals due to its semi-anonymous and decentralized characteristics. It gives opportunities for money laundering and illegal fundraising, abusing the system by hacking and taking advantage of vulnerable and not experienced people.

At the same time, the fact that all transactions are recorded gives the opportunity to track activities and provide estimates of how much is associated with crime. For example, Chainalysis in its 2020 Crypto Crime report shows that the share of illicit cryptocurrency rose in 2019 to reach 1.1 per cent of all activities (around US$11 billion) (Chainalysis, 2020).

For regulators, it is important to keep tracking the development of illicit activities and consider the main trends in this area, which include the following:

(a) The majority of criminal activities in cryptocurrency are associated with a small segment of white-collar criminals. Thus, individuals with access to privileged information and their activities may need to be under special supervision.

[49] See https://digitales.wien.gv.at/site/en/projekt/culture-token/.

[50] Contribution from the Government of Austria, available at https://unctad.org/system/files/non-official-document/CSTD_2020-21_c01_HB_Austria_en.pdf.

[51] Contribution from the Government of the Russian Federation, available at https://unctad.org/system/files/non-official-document/CSTD_2020-21_c25_B_Russia_en.pdf.

[52] Contribution from the Government of Switzerland, available at https://unctad.org/system/files/non-official-document/CSTD_ 2020-21_c29_B_Switzerland_en.pdf.

(b) Money-laundering is crucial for cryptocurrency crime as all criminals need to convert holdings into cash. Understanding the work of sophisticated services and networks designed for money-laundering and their interaction with criminals may help in the choice of effective policies to deal with it.

(c) Scams make most of cryptocurrency-related crime, accounting for almost US$9 billion in 2019. Thus, consumer protection should be one of regulators' priority; currency exchanges can play a crucial role in informing and protecting the public.

As blockchain technology evolves, cryptocrime will likely continue to evolve in both scope and technological sophistication. Some trends in the future may include using more non-custodial mixers, using chain hopping (swapping one type of cryptocurrency for another to obfuscate the path of funds) as an alternative to mixing, use of privacy coins by criminals due to higher anonymity and increasing the anonymity of P2P exchange options.

3. Inequality

As in other areas, the connection between blockchain and inequality cannot be described unequivocally. There are several channels, through which inequality is affected, in various direction. The final effect may depend on public policies acknowledging and leveraging the use of such channels.

Opportunities provided by cryptocurrencies are fully enjoyed by only a few due to the cost of access, complexity, etc. Statistics show that inequality among cryptocurrency holders is notoriously high. According to bitinfo,[53] considering the total number and value of various cryptocurrencies holders, 50 per cent of all bitcoin addresses hold less than 0.01 bitcoin and almost 90 per cent hold less than 1 BTC; 95 per cent of coins are held by only 3 per cent of all addresses (figure 9).

[53] See https://bitinfocharts.com/top-100-richest-bitcoin-addresses.html.

Figure 9
Share of coins and addresses by balance
(Percentage)

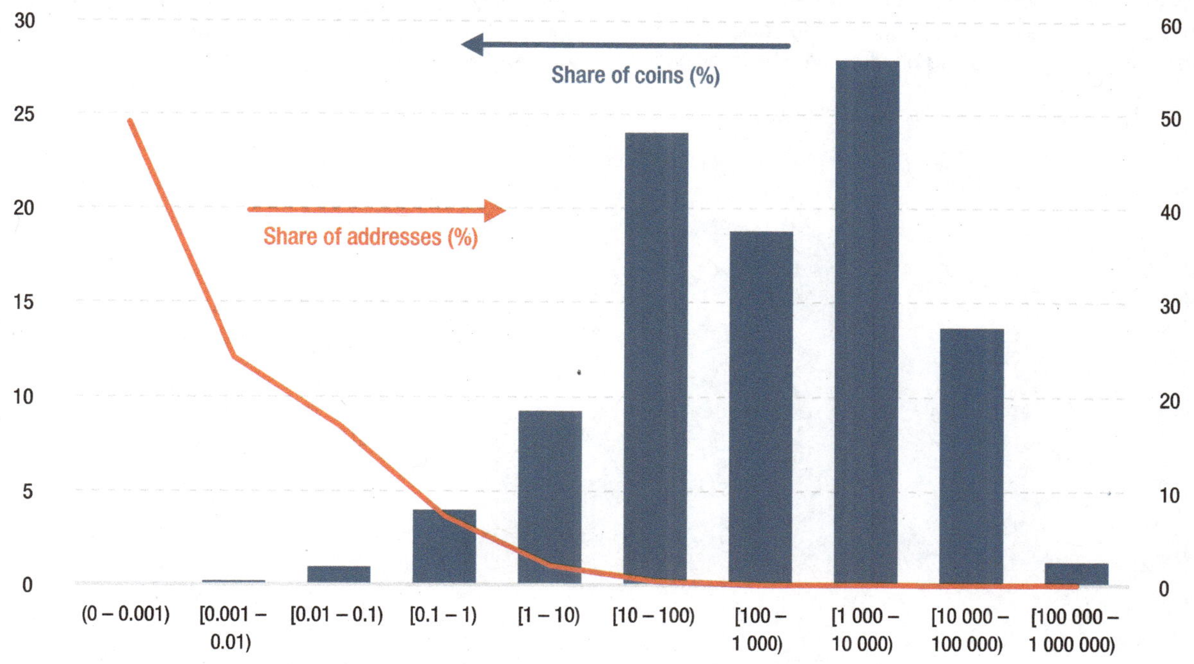

Source: UNCTAD, based on Bitinfo, October 2020.

At the same time, several blockchain applications could help to reduce inequality. Some examples from various regions of the world are listed below:

- Blockchain micro-lending applicationss have been introduced in South-East Asia to help people get a credit history on the blockchain. In 2018, 1.7 billion unbanked people could be potentially reached by these applicationss (Carter, 2020).
- In 2017, US$5 million worth of bitcoin were donated to a charity organization in Kenya that was helping people to get access to clean water and was sending direct payments to people in poverty, helping with food and other living expenses and school tuition (Cheong, 2020).
- Blockchain technology can help to connect directly with the public for fundraising with Initial Coin Offerings (ICOs). The ability to tokenize and portion out ownership of any asset class, such as real estate, art etc., can open financial opportunities for middle- and lower-class consumers.

4. Privacy

Privacy is another issue at the centre of the debate when deploying blockchain in different applications. Privacy in blockchain can imply the ability to perform transactions without leaking identification information, still allowing the user to remain compliant. Despite the fact that transactions and data are authenticated through cryptography, it is possible to access the data, including, in some applications using blockchain, the information on the identities of the parties in the transactions; this thus causes a threat to personal privacy. With the rise and widespread adoption of this technology, data breaches could become frequent. In particular, nodes in public blockchains have direct access to the data in the blockchain, and in the absence of clear regulations, it may cause significant business risks.

The most significant cases of blockchain privacy failure include the hacking of theMtGox Bitcoin exchange in 2014, when hackers were able to steal US$450 million in Bitcoin and were not identified. The Coinbase cryptocurrency exchange was attacked in 2012; personal email addresses were used to change verification numbers, allowing hackers to access wallets. DAO was hacked in 2016; hackers stole up to US$100 million, according to some estimates. Hackings often occur as discussed in the section above ("Criminal activities"); while the magnitude of hackings has declined, the potential loss is significant.

At the same time, blockchain technology, due to data transparency and integrity features, can improve privacy by verifying and managing consent; providing individuals with clear notifications and records of personal data usage across distributed systems and minimizing data sharing between data controllers and their processors. Some researchers suggest that self-governing blockchain-enabled identity and data management solutions can provide the preferred way to maintain and demonstrate data privacy. For now, it is important for policymakers to better tailor data privacy laws, regulations and guidance for blockchain use cases.

V. HARNESSING BLOCKCHAIN FOR SUSTAINABLE DEVELOPMENT

This chapter discusses the challenges that Governments face and what they should do to influence the rate and direction of innovation and competence building in blockchain to contribute to their national development priorities and accelerate the progress towards the Sustainable Development Goals.

One of the challenges that most developing countries continue to face is to counteract the effects of the global concentration dynamics in the production and development of technology. Blockchain innovations are no exception. While this does not prevent Governments from leveraging blockchain to accelerate their progress towards the Sustainable Development Goals, it does have significant implications in the associated costs of such an undertaking. The most crucial challenge is then to promote competence building in blockchain in such a way that a country develops the capacity to use, but also to create customized versions suited to their conditions and needs.

Another critical challenge is the misconception of what new technologies can do. For many, blockchain still represents an abstract technology with unclear benefits. It is generally believed that technology is about bringing full transparency to transactions. Blockchain can do this if required, but it is not entirely true that everything will be transparent. Another misconception is that it only serves for traceability purposes. The challenge is to build awareness of what blockchain is and what problems it can solve if correctly implemented. Many start-ups are trying to sell off the shelf solutions to governments without a sound assessment of whether the physical system is ready to be put into a blockchain and without an adequate return on investment assessment.

Blockchain regulations will require concerted efforts for both establishing and enforcing rules. Blockchain-based systems that are part of a global network further increase the complexity. In systems that are powered by the combined computational power of nodes with different geographical locations, under various legislations, and where there is no central party governing and operating the system, who should be held responsible and accountable for misbehaviour or failure? Alternatively, how can liability be apportioned? The challenge for developing countries is two-fold: first, to increase their engagement with global digital governance; second, to simultaneously develop national capabilities to develop and enforce regulations for blockchain.

Similarly, blockchain is still in incipient stages of standardization and continuously surrounded by highly contested terminology. Standardization will be an essential step towards more comprehensive regulatory frameworks. Currently, the problem is twofold. On the one hand, the lack of regulation limits the capacity of Governments to cope with fraud, local regulatory compliance and tax evasion. On the other, it hinders technology adoption and innovation, primarily affecting entrepreneurs and start-ups, which are often confronted with the uncertainty of being incurring a legal problem.

The lack of standardization among blockchains can be the source of additional problems related to interoperability. For example, the costs of integrating blockchains into financial infrastructures like payment and settlement systems require not only industry-wide coordination and collaboration but also demands significant expenses. Systems integration problems related to legacy systems are not an exclusive challenge of developed countries. To a different extent, though, Governments in developing countries are also confronted with the challenge of ensuring that blockchain systems can be integrated with the existing infrastructure, yet often incompatible systems.

The discussion in the following section present policy recommendations covering two main areas: (a) building capacities for strengthening the national ecosystem for blockchain innovation; and (b) creating the regulatory environment for support blockchain innovation, while addressing potential risks.

A. BUILDING CAPACITIES FOR STRENGTHENING THE NATIONAL SYSTEM FOR BLOCKCHAIN INNOVATION

National innovation systems determine the rate and direction of innovation in a country. The following sections provide recommendations for and examples related to countries at different levels of development, in recognition that their innovations systems have characteristics that require targeted policy advice. However, it is essential to note that this is a presentation choice and that each recommendation is also relevant to countries at different levels of development.

The discussion will focus on the following areas:

- Low and lower-middle-income developing countries: build the basic human capacity and infrastructure, and start pilot projects, that could kickstart the diffusion of blockchain.
- Upper-middle-income country: facilitate the linkages of their national innovation system with the global ecosystem of innovation in blockchain to create opportunities for their firms to engage, contribute and benefit from the development of the technology and the rapid pace of innovation.
- High-income countries: develop legal and policy frameworks that allow organizations and the public to benefit from blockchain technology while minimizing its risks and protecting users.

1. Low- and lower-middle-income developing countries

With numerous benefits that could come from the use of blockchain technology, low and lower-middle-income developing countries also face several challenges given their prevailing policy framework, state of infrastructure for digital tools and quality of human resource for technological advancement. The challenges of poor and costly internet service, unstable and sometimes non-existent electricity as well as lack of know-how are incredibly daunting in the deployment and utilization of blockchain technology and must be addressed for any meaningful leverage of the technology in these countries.

Low and lower-middle-income developing countries' ability to overcome these challenges, could mean a chance for a leap in areas of financial inclusion, financial technology, e-governance (including digital IDs, taxation), international trade, interoperability IT systems and digitization of supply chains. Countries where efficiency and trust are low can benefit the most from blockchains. However, the technical infrastructure needs to be assessed and the system requirements specified for a technical upgrade where appropriate, which can be pricey, especially for economies with limited financial resources such as the least developed countries. In that context, many member States will seek financing from donors, making donor coordination a pivotal aspect to success.

For low-income countries, harnessing blockchain technology will first require the development of digital infrastructure and skill training. The process must incorporate STEM education, cross-linkages between research and commerce, fast technological adoption in the industry and the development of pilot projects that showcase the value of blockchain technology. Although cryptocurrencies are still the most frequent implementation of the technology, low- and lower-middle-income developing countries can also benefit from blockchain applications in manufacturing, health care, energy and Government. To develop technological capacity, Governments must encourage innovation and create opportunities for skill development, for example, in cryptography, data structures and web development for advances in blockchain adoption. An effective policy platform will combine enhanced STEM training, bilateral collaborations and knowledge transfers, operational support infrastructure, and financial investment in blockchain pilot projects.

Identify and form groups of blockchain experts

Blockchain being a nascent technology, the expertise required for implementing blockchain at scale will not be readily available in low- and lower-middle-income developing countries. Governments could identify and invite experts in law and technology, with various degrees of expertise in blockchain, from academia and industry to join an advisory board. This advisory board would inform the regulatory process and develop strategies to attract technical talent and investment in blockchain ventures. For example, South Africa has established a partnership between research, industry and Government called SANBA to develop blockchain implementation in the South African context.[54] Similarly, other countries can benefit from the expertise of an advisory board to guide policy framework, content knowledge and technical infrastructure for digital Government.

Invest in research institutions and graduate programs in advanced STEM fields

Investing in education is a crucial step to increase the rate of adoption of blockchain and other frontier technologies. Universities should be incentivized to improve training on cryptography, data structures, software infrastructure and web development,

[54] See https://cointelegraph.com/news/south-african-national-blockchain-alliance-holds-online-launch.

along with other related fields related to Blockchain technology. Increasing research capacity will support the training of practitioners and experts who understand and implement blockchain. The link between research, young talent and industry can be further facilitated by research institutions, hackathons and job fairs. For example, Australia[55] and Malaysia[56] have established research institutes to provide a low-stakes environment for firms and researchers to experiment with blockchain solutions, and the city of Daegu in the Republic of Korea is reported to have allocated $6 million to promote blockchain and artificial intelligence education.[57] As a first step, public universities should acquire the required technical equipment and hire skilled personnel. Grants, scholarships and competitive awards can inspire talent development and help universities develop qualified practitioners.

Establish associations, laboratories, incubators and consultancies for the blockchain industry

The development of the blockchain in lower-middle-income countries can be better facilitated with active support services focused on blockchain. For example, national blockchain associations and laboratories play a relevant role in the innovation and development of blockchain (see box 8 for examples from countries of different levels of development). The Goal is to build core capacity not only in the technology itself, but also the policy implications, economic impact and regulatory frameworks. The process could be initiated by the advisory board, aided by the relevant ministries, that assesses the best use cases of Blockchain technology in the context of the respective country. For countries which have more mature technological industries, organizing international cooperation projects that are blockchain focused will accelerate the rate of successful deployment and facilitate knowledge transfers. These consultancy services can support initial developments in blockchain technology within Government and the private sector, providing technical, organizational and managerial services.

Box 8
National blockchain associations and laboratories

Cuba. Since 2017, the Cryptography Institute of the Faculty of Mathematics and Computing of the University of Habana in Cuba investigates the potentials of blockchain technology, with the aim of evaluating and assessing the possible applications of this technology in the country. The results obtained to date have been made available to the Business Group on Informatics and Communications (GEIC), the Central Bank of Cuba and the Union of Jurists.[58]

Kenya. In October 2017, the Blockchain Association of Kenya was established as a non-profit organization under the Societies Act Cap 12 Laws of Kenya to promote the adoption of blockchain and cryptocurrency technology in Kenya and East Africa by building a network of competent homegrown human capital.[59]

Latvia. In 2017, the Latvian Blockchain Association was established to promote the research and deployment of blockchain technology.[60]

Romania. A blockchain hub in Romania, Modex Blockchain Labs, is devoted to blockchain development. It is a blockchain database company that innovates to solve the last mile adoption problem of the blockchain. It offers services for the entire blockchain technology ecosystem: marketplace for smart contracts, community tools for developers, and Blockchain Database solutions for enterprises.[61]

Saudi Arabia. Saudi Arabia is committed to establish a Blockchain Laboratory to test and experiment with ideas and solutions to develop and enhance the Government's procedural services, and to come up with a plan that will improve the quality of government services provided to citizens using Blockchain technology.[62]

Source: UNCTAD, based on contributions from the Governments of Cuba, Kenya, Latvia, Romania and Saudi Arabia, available at https://unctad.org/meeting/commission-science-and-technology-development-twenty-fourth-session.

[55] See https://www.coindesk.com/austrian-government-backs-new-blockchain-research-institute.

[56] See https://www.coinspeaker.com/magic-with-mba-has-launched-blockchain-researcher-lab-program-in-malaysia/.

[57] See https://cointelegraph.com/news/this-south-korean-city-is-spending-millions-to-turn-people-into-blockchain-experts.

[58] Contribution from the Government of Cuba, available at https://unctad.org/system/files/non-official-document/CSTD_2020-21_c04_HB_Cuba_es.pdf.

[59] Contribution from the Government of Kenya, available at https://unctad.org/system/files/non-official-document/CSTD_2020-21_c17_HB_Kenya_en.pdf.

[60] Contribution from the Government of Latvia, available at https://unctad.org/system/files/non-official-document/CSTD_2020-21_c21_B_Latvia_en.pdf.

[61] Contribution from the Government of Romania, available at https://unctad.org/system/files/non-official-document/CSTD_2020-21_c24_HB_Romania_en.pdf, and https://modex.tech/.

[62] Contribution from the Government of Saudi Arabia, available at https://unctad.org/system/files/non-official-document/CSTD_2020-21_c27_B_Saudi%20Arabia_en.pdf.

Establish pilot programmes to build trust in blockchain technology:

Initiating pilot programmes through public services can be an opportunity to experiment with blockchain solutions and demonstrate its value. For instance, Kenya has implemented its first blockchain and smart-contract based retail bond M-Akiba, a government bond which can be purchased without a bank account.[63] M-Akiba accounts are easy to set up quickly with mobile phones, and minimum investments are comparatively low ($28 approximately), making it accessible to a large number of unbanked users. Blockchain and smart contracts allow M-Akiba to manage a large number of small transactions with low overhead costs. There are also several examples of blockchain use case developed in Uganda, including a free zone to focus on blockchain and emerging technologies, the use of blockchain to identify counterfeit drugs and to prevent their distribution in the pharmaceutical supply chain, and projects on blockchain in the agri-food value chain (see box 9).

The pilot project does not necessarily have to involve digital payment systems and value chains. Other examples include data-sharing between departments, verifying bids in public contracts, or creating a public data portal. Once a successful project is launched, more initiatives will learn from its challenges and develop institutional knowledge in blockchain implementation.

63 https://www.coindesk.com/world-bank-to-support-blockchain-bonds-trial-in-kenya

Box 9
Blockchain use cases in Uganda

In September 2019, the Uganda Free Zones Authority issued a licence for the establishment of a free zone to focus on blockchain and emerging technologies to Blockchain Technologies Ltd., and its parent company CryptoSavannah.[64] Uganda is the first country in Africa to issue this type of license. The free zone will contribute to establishing Uganda as the continental leader in blockchain and other Fourth Industrial Revolution (4IR) technologies. The Government hopes to combat the sale and distribution of counterfeit pharmaceuticals in Uganda and the EAC. The contracted MediConnect blockchain-based platform enables the recording of prescription medication, thus identifying counterfeit drugs and preventing their distribution in the pharmaceutical supply chain. According to the Ugandan National Drug Authority, 10 per cent of prescribed medications have counterfeits on the market.[65]

FAO and Ministry of Agriculture, Animal Industry and Fisheries of Uganda (MAAIF) have started another pilot project aiming to increase knowledge and improve the capacity of blockchain technology for agri-food value chain development for stakeholders in public and private sectors in Uganda, including policymakers and those representing smallholder farmers, SMEs, women, youth and rural communities.

Some specific objectives and activities include: (a) identifying key areas of blockchain applications (e.g., supply chain management, certification, food safety, smart contracts and e-commerce) and key-value chains for blockchain applications, and provide recommendations for adopting blockchain and related technologies for agri-food value chain development in Uganda; (b) developing a training programme for blockchain and related technologies for agri-food value chain development with relevant use cases and companies invited to share experiences and carry out training and various consultations, and overall to increase knowledge and build the capacity of stakeholders in public and private sectors; (c) disseminating findings and recommendations and promoting experience sharing through webinars and workshops and knowledge products; and (d) engaging stakeholders through a participatory approach and promoting synergies of stakeholders and initiatives as well as partnerships and investment and innovation opportunities to ensure sustainable impacts.[66]

In other sectors, the South African coffee trader Carico Café Connoisseur, which trades quality Ugandan coffees like Bugisu Blue, has started tracking and tracing exports using blockchain technology.[67] A cryptocurrency exchange, Binance Uganda, has been active since June 2018[68] and has, to date, 40,000 registered users.[69] With its large young and unbanked population, Uganda is seen as having potential for the deployment of cryptocurrencies. However, the Ministry of Finance has advised parliament that it is working on introducing regulations to govern cryptocurrencies, as there have been reports on the emergence of pyramid schemes branding themselves as crypto projects, with the usual consequences for naïve speculators.[70]

Source: UNCTAD and contributions from FAO, available at https://unctad.org/system/files/non-official-document/CSTD_2020-21_c11_B_FAO_en.pdf.

64 www.unlock-bc.com/news/2019-09-17/uganda-announces-blockchain-freezone.

65 cointelegraph.com/news/uganda-to-deploy-mediconnects-blockchain-platform-for-tracing-fake-drugs.

66 Contribution from FAO, available at https://unctad.org/system/files/non-official-document/CSTD_2020-21_c11_B_FAO_en.pdf.

67 See http://www.reuters.com/article/us-uganda-coffee/ugandan-firm-uses-blockchain-to-trace-coffee-from-farms-to-stores-idUSKCN1PH1ZW.

68 See http://support.binance.co.ug/hc/en-us/articles/360006720911-Official-Launch-of-Binance-Uganda-Fiat-Crypto-Exchange.

69 See http://cryptobriefing.com/uganda-blockchain-hub/.

70 Ibid.

Integrate blockchain-based services to existing platforms

Pilot projects can help promote blockchain applications and get users and builders interested in the technology's potential. However, using blockchain to enhance existing digital service can be more achievable, and at times more useful, than creating new applications. The Government, aided by the advisory board, can assess where the technology could be relevant, appropriate and best used in the active digital services and implement integration projects to make digital services faster, more cost-effective, and more secure. India, Georgia and Ghana are working to incorporate blockchain-based land-registry databases within existing land title systems. The immutability of blockchain ledgers suits the challenge of solving land disputes using falsified documents. In Turkey, a project is being implemented on the use of blockchain technology in digital identification systems to promote understanding and demonstrate the benefits of the technology (box 10).

Box 10
Turkey: Blockchain-based Next Generation Decentralized Digital Identity Infrastructure

In Turkey, the National Research Institute of Electronics and Cryptology (TÜBITAK BILGEM UEKAE) is working on the Blockchain-based Next Generation Decentralized Digital Identity Infrastructure (MODKA). This infrastructure will be integrated with existing identity systems and other infrastructures so that it can be used as the future national digital identity management backbone of Turkey. The MODKA will be prepared for the Internet of things (IoT) by drawing the framework of digital identity life cycles for legal entities. Blockchain technology will be combined with the cryptographic and e-identity expertise of TÜBITAK. All components needed within the scope of the digital identity ecosystem are developed at the prototype level. When MODKA is put into use on a national scale, it will pave the way for many structural transformations with the leading role it will assume in the electronic transformation of national information systems.

Source: UNCTAD, based on contributions from the Government of Turkey, available at https://unctad.org/system/files/non-official-document/CSTD_2020-21_c33_B_Turkey_en.pdf.

2. Upper-middle-income developing countries

Although blockchain is still in the early stages of adoption in many upper-middle-income countries, it is more likely that these countries have the technical foundation and the human resources for rapid technological adoption. Most regulation around blockchain in upper-middle-income countries are still undecided. The challenge for many of these countries is to connect the domestic innovation system and the global ecosystem of innovation, so blockchain practitioners can be technologically and organizationally prepared to benefit from blockchain technology. The rapid pace of change in the technology itself and the long timeframe that such capacity development demands call for strategic and concerted efforts to build capabilities in the blockchain-related areas. There is considerable potential for blockchain applications to integrate with existing digital infrastructure and create value through inclusion and expansion unachievable through traditional digital services.

Establish a national blockchain strategy

Defining the policy objectives regarding blockchain technology in a national strategy is necessary for long-term planning and coordinated development. It will define a Government's vision for blockchain to investors and businesses, therefore clarifying the regulatory stance, eliminating ambiguity regarding public development and avoiding patchwork regulations at different levels of Government. A national strategy will also clearly identify how blockchain could contribute to the national priorities and the role it will play in the public and private sector (see box 11). Regulatory bodies can take steps to understand the technology and its use cases in cryptocurrencies, smart contracts, databases and supply chains to devise sector-specific regulatory frameworks. A national strategy can also establish necessary ethical standards and emphasize the principles along which blockchain applications will be built. It will also survey the landscape for blockchain development and identify advanced and emerging sectors. The process will enable the Government and the private sector to work together through the techno-economic transition, create signposts for future development and ease blockchain adoption for both the public and private sectors.

Blockchain incubators, innovation hubs and networks

Alongside investing in public education in science and technology, establishing research institutions, innovation hubs and blockchain focused incubators and networks can accelerate the rate of adoption of blockchain applications and innovation to overcome the technology's current challenges. For example, in Turkey, the Blockchain and Research Network (BAG) platform has been established to facilitate research and development activities on blockchain technology. The BAG platform aims at increasing national know-how rapidly by enabling researchers to work in various fields of blockchain to develop fruitful projects together by combining their efforts and using resource more effectively.

Box 11
National strategies for blockchain development

Countries are committed to develop and implement national strategies to promote the long-term development of blockchain and its uses, through innovation and pilot applications, and close cooperation between the private and public sectors for best results.

Kenya. The Government of Kenya possesses a strong history with respect to the involvement in and prioritization of digital agendas. The willingness of Kenya to embrace innovation in partnership with the private sector has earned the country the moniker of "Africa's Silicon Savannah". This innovative, forward-leaning approach to national development is reflected in the Big Four Agenda of Kenya, which will be supported and enhanced by leveraging emerging technologies. The Big Four Agenda focuses on food and nutrition security, affordable housing, enhancing manufacturing and universal health coverage.[71]

Russian Federation. Blockchain technology development is a part of the activities provided for by the federal project Digital Technologies under the National project Digital Economy of the Russian Federation. Blockchain technology is also mentioned in the Strategy of Information Society Development in the Russian Federation for the period of 2017–2030. A road map for developing the "end-to-end" digital technology of "distributed register system" was drawn. The road map envisages the use of blockchain in industry, finance, logistics and Government. According to the road map, all State information systems are planned to be transferred to blockchain.[72]

Saudi Arabia. Saudi Arabia adopted "Vision 2030" as a road map for economic growth and national development; it involves public, private and non-profit sectors rolling out an integrated governance model established by the Council of Ministers. The national strategy aims at adopting advanced technologies for the greater good of the country. A relevant initiative is to develop a Blockchain Laboratory with the aim of testing and experimenting with ideas and solutions to develop and enhance the Government's procedural services, and to come up with a plan that will improve the quality of government services provided to citizens using blockchain technology.[73]

Thailand. To harness the potential of the fourth industrial revolution, Thailand has implemented a number of policies known as Thailand 4.0 – a visionary scheme to transform the country into a value-based and innovation-driven economy. In keeping with Thailand 4.0's emphasis on the use of digital technologies to spur national economic growth and development, local blockchain start-ups have a critical role to play as catalysts for the promotion of digital innovation in Thailand. Leading by example, the Government of Thailand is experimenting with using distributed ledgers in the operations of its various State agencies. The Government has identified three main blockchain project areas (in transport and logistics, banking and finance, and digital identity) that could also be valuable cases for other blockchain players in South-East Asia.[74]

Turkey. Blockchain has been a national priority in Turkey. The Eleventh Development Plan (2019–2023) states that blockchain-based digital central bank money will be implemented, and it is planned that processes and technological infrastructure will be improved to utilize new technologies such as big data, cloud computing, mobile platforms, the Internet of things, artificial intelligence and blockchain in the development of public services (e.g. e-government). Furthermore, as emphasized in the 2023 Industry and Technology Strategy developed by the Ministry of Industry and Technology, the development of the national blockchain infrastructure will be encouraged to create a blockchain-based network.[75]

Source: UNCTAD, based on contributions from the Governments of Kenya, the Russian Federation, Saudi Arabia, Thailand and Turkey, available at https://unctad.org/meeting/commission-science-and-technology-development-twenty-fourth-session.

---

[71] Contribution from the Government of Kenya available at https://unctad.org/system/files/non-official-document/CSTD_2020-21_c17_HB_Kenya_en.pdf.

[72] Contribution from the Government of the Russian Federation available at https://unctad.org/system/files/non-official-document/CSTD_2020-21_c25_B_Russia_en.pdf.

[73] Contribution from the Government of Saudi Arabia available at https://unctad.org/system/files/non-official-document/CSTD_2020-21_c27_B_Saudi%20Arabia_en.pdf.

[74] Contribution from the Government of Thailand available at https://unctad.org/system/files/non-official-document/CSTD_2020-21_c30_B_Thailand_en.pdf.

[75] Contribution from the Government of Turkey available at https://unctad.org/system/files/non-official-document/CSTD_2020-21_c33_B_Turkey_en.pdf.

These institutions can become the ground zero for building technical knowledge and accelerate the development of enterprise-ready applications. Research institutions can also boost general understanding of blockchain technology, and trust in its applications, and provide an environment for experimentation and design testing. Japan,[76] Malaysia[77] and Singapore[78] have gone further and created sandbox policy environments to test the limits of blockchain technology, especially cryptocurrencies, and its interactions with other digital systems.[79]

Specialized blockchain task force

Upper-middle-income countries can develop a multi-stakeholder blockchain task force to develop expertise in blockchain technology and policy. Certain countries have existing working groups, such as the federation of banks (FEBRABAN) of Brazil, which is tasked with examining Blockchain and its impact on the banking sector.[80] The focus of these task forces will be to develop a technical understanding of Blockchain within the Government and monitor international developments in the technology. It will prepare the Government for understanding the regulatory practices for Blockchain as well as identify potentially harmful cryptofinancial activity. The taskforce can also verify whether blockchain usage is necessary for specific tasks and whether easier ways to accomplish the tasks are available.

Develop blockchain guidelines and principles

Government stakeholders can develop best practices and foundational principles to guide the development of blockchain integration. The guidelines will define the kind of operations that can benefit from blockchain solutions and those that are more suitable for traditional digital services. The above-mentioned task force can direct the development of the guidelines and principles. The task force can also delineate the attributes of different blockchain systems (e.g. private versus public) and suggest the best-use cases for each system.

Deciding on the guiding principles can signal future developments in the regulatory space such as policies governing privacy and interoperability. For example, the principle to uphold technology neutrality – policies that ensure a level playing field for all commercial entities using blockchain technology – will promote a more equitable business environment. The principles should ideally guide regulation to be permissive rather than restrictive, to build trust and invite innovation while creating the enforcement capacity to prevent harm to users. Blockchain principles can also guide regulation for cryptocurrencies, taxation, the legal status of smart contracts and supply chain management, among other applications.

Establish standards for interoperability

With various blockchain services operating in tandem, establishing common encryption and data standards can facilitate interoperability and create ecosystems where blockchain services work together to provide greater value. Establishing standards will build resilience in applications and reduce the risk of a fragmented blockchain ecosystem (with potential disadvantages such as vendor lock-in). Accessible blockchain ecosystems will lower the barrier to entry for new ventures and encourage investment in the technology. However, setting standards that are too rigid, and are enforced before the technology has stabilized, will result in expensive transitions in the future. Governments will need to balance promoting the establishment of standards for faster adoption, while being flexible enough to account for rapid changes in technology and how it is used.

Identify key use cases and form strategic collaborations

Taking a long-term view, policymakers can identify key areas where blockchain applications can provide real value through public services. The Indian public think-tank Niti Aayog has identified areas where Blockchain technology can build on the public digital infrastructure of India.[81] In Thailand, the Office of the Courts of Justice is reported to have plans to use DTL to manage court records and other judicial information by 2021.[82] National-level assessments can identify potential use cases of blockchain technology and set short to medium-term milestones. Once identified, the

[76] See https://www.forbes.com/sites/japan/2019/06/26/japans-blockchain-sandbox-is-paving-the-way-for-the-fintech-future/#254e5ac93279.

[77] See https://www.researchgate.net/publication/338304841_Regulating_FinTech_Businesses_The_Malaysian_Experience.

[78] See https://www.mas.gov.sg/development/fintech/sandbox.

[79] See https://cointelegraph.com/news/south-koreas-fintech-sandbox-creates-380-new-blockchain-jobs.

[80] See https://www.rvo.nl/sites/default/files/2018/02/brazils-beginning-blockchain-business.pdf.

[81] See https://niti.gov.in/sites/default/files/2020-01/Blockchain_The_India_Strategy_Part_I.pdf.

[82] See https://dailyhodl.com/2020/08/22/thailand-judicial-system-planning-big-shift-to-blockchain-will-migrate-records-to-distributed-ledger/.

use cases can be achieved with international and local partners with technical expertise. For example, IBM is working in India[83] and South Africa[84] to establish blockchain-based industrial supply chain systems. As different use-cases are developed, partnerships can increase the rate of knowledge transfer and build successful models for blockchain integration. Implementing blockchain in public services will signal institutional endorsement that will generate interest and trust in the technology.

Establish channels of collaboration with the international community

Countries face similar challenges to develop a climate of innovation. Creating and participating in forums where international and local practitioners can meet and share their work will provide opportunities for collaboration and learning. Supporting blockchain experts, policymakers and technologists to attend conferences and training opportunities will create better linkages between the local innovation ecosystem and the international community working on blockchain applications. Governments can set up scholarships for students in domestic and foreign universities working on frontier technologies. These initiatives, over time, will advance the system of innovation and develop the professional force that can use blockchain technology to its full potential.

3. High-income countries

For high-income countries, demand for blockchain services has increased significantly in recent years. Countries have made important inroads, not only in increasing the technological potential of blockchain, but also in creating an environment that can support blockchain applications. International competition may bring blockchain technology to more user-friendly services, and high-income countries may stand to benefit most from the first wave of consumer-ready applications. However, questions regarding interoperability, scalability, privacy and transparency, and regulation remain unanswered, and the rate of change of the technology is as rapid as the results are uncertain. High-income countries should look to develop legal and policy frameworks that allow the real economy and the public to benefit from blockchain technology, while minimizing its risks and protecting users.

Establish a blockchain development committee

Business leaders and policymakers must communicate with each other to understand, innovate, regulate, and implement blockchain technology effectively. A blockchain development committee can perform as a high-level forum where decisionmakers can communicate with stakeholders and identify viable pathways for Blockchain development. Like previous suggestions on Blockchain task forces and expert groups, the committee will have similar objectives of studying the development of Blockchain technology in other countries, identifying use cases, advising public projects and developing the regulatory guidelines in consultation with the private sector. However, the committee should also have the mandate to actively support blockchain's growth within the Government through task forces in charge of specific use cases, research and advisory services. The committee can oversee the national blockchain road map and develop cross-sectoral linkages between a Government and the private sector.

Synergy through research and development

Although all countries have national innovations systems, high-income countries have the funding and human resources that increase the chance of breakthrough innovations in technology and implementation. In this regard, grants and financial incentives by Governments should have the role of creating incentives for innovations in the blockchain that contribute to the Sustainable Development Goals. Government support for new ventures can ease this burden and allow more experimental applications to mature (see box 12 for an example from Portugal). A Government could set up competitive grants for innovative new businesses and provide institutional support. For new technologies, it is often the case that the costs of development are borne by few actors while the benefits are enjoyed by many. With Government sharing the risks, the burden of innovation can be eased for private firms. For example, the Government of the United States set up US$800,000 grants for firms working on anti-forgery blockchain solutions in 2018.[85] Besides monetary support, setting up laboratories and regulatory sandboxes (elaborated below) for experimentation can further encourage innovation.

[83] See https://papers.ssrn.com/sol3/papers.cfm?abstract_id=3265654.

[84] See http://www.engineeringnews.co.za/article/ibm-in-broad-partnership-to-develop-supply-chain-blockchain-2019-02-22.

[85] See https://www.coindesk.com/us-government-offering-up-to-800k-for-anti-forgery-blockchain-solutions.

Box 12
GovTech: Using blockchain to support the Sustainable Development Goals in Portugal

GovTech is a Portuguese public competition that rewards innovative products and services provided by start-ups and addressing at least one of the 17 Sustainable Development Goals. GovTech was designed had two main goals in mind: to promote the Goals nationwide, and to stimulate the startup ecosystem and dynamism in Portugal. Start-ups usually employ young people and have a reputation for being disruptive, creative and innovative, enabling their development and teaching them about the importance of the Sustainable Development Goals, promotes a sustained, inclusive and sustainable growth. In the first edition held in 2018, there were 113 projects focusing on the environment, women's rights, the youth, migrants, fighting poverty and so on.[86]

The use of blockchain in the voting phase opened to the public was one of the perks of this competition. To make the vote a more interesting process, a virtual coin based on blockchain technology was created, named GovTechs. Participants could vote on their preferred projects by investing with GovTechs on the website; this insured the security and transparency of all participatory process. The projects selected were Intelligent Forest Management Technologies, Green Salt and Healthy Life for All and Bio2Skin.[87] The use of blockchain in the voting process served as a learning process for the Government of Portugal as it was the first time a governmental initiative used blockchain, so the Goal was also to test the potential of this emergent technology and have some lessons learned that can now be used in future projects.[88]

Source: UNCTAD, based on contributions from the Government of Portugal, available at available at https://unctad.org/system/files/non-official-document/CSTD_2020-21_c23_B_Portugal_en.pdf.

Create innovation incentives, support for new ventures and jobs

Through research investment, support for startups, academic scholarships, hackathons and workshops, high-income countries can also attract and foster the national blockchain ecosystem and develop the future workforce of blockchain. Just as computer science had few practitioners a few decades ago, the blockchain community is currently small. Through better job opportunities, more people will consider a career in blockchain development and advance the field over time. For example, the blockchain ecosystem in Latvia is highly dynamic and innovative with strong support from the Government and active engagement of stakeholders in the private sector (box 13).

High-income countries should also incentivize the research and development required to tackle the limitations in blockchain technology: the speed of verification, energy consumption, network security, among others. Innovations within the technology will eventually translate to greater usability and incorporation of blockchain into everyday digital services. Countries that can solve these challenges will be the first to benefit from improved efficiency and will be able to establish standards that are adopted globally.

Box 13
Blockchain's supportive business climate in Latvia

Latvia incentivizes local blockchain start-ups through a flexible tax system, tax benefits for early companies with the need for funding, and issues special visas for the founders to become residents in the country. Latvia scores third place in the OECD rankings for the attractiveness of the tax system and has the lowest financial requirements for start-up founders. StartUpLatvia is a government-supported initiative for further fostering the ecosystem. In 2018, the Action Plan for the Development of Start-up Ecosystem was adopted in Latvia. One of its main objectives is to raise public awareness and promote cooperation between start-ups and the academic sector and corporations. Since 2019, more focus has been brought towards the cooperation between start-ups and ICT companies, State-owned companies, corporations and other public sector bodies.

Latvia has also leveraged its highly qualified and skilled pool of thousands of IT professionals and software developers – out of a 1.9 million population, 30,000 people are employed in IT. Foreign companies have been outsourcing their IT projects in Latvia for the past years, and software development outsourcing plays a crucial role in the country's exports. Latvia has around 6,500 ICT companies and over 400 start-ups. Many of them have already started specializing in blockchain-based development and offer full service to outsource. AXIOMA Group, Blockvis, Netcore and Soft-FX are some of the most widely known blockchain development companies that have served Binance, Bitfinex, Bitstamp, Kraken and many other big names in the industry.

Source: UNCTAD, based on contribution from the Government of Latvia available at https://unctad.org/system/files/non-official-document/CSTD_2020-21_c21_B_Latvia_en.pdf.

Establish regulatory sandboxes

Regulatory sandboxes are special regulatory allowances to test an innovation under the supervision of regulators.

[86] See www.govtech.gov.pt.

[87] Contribution from the Government of Portugal available at https://unctad.org/system/files/non-official-document/CSTD_2020-21_c23_B_Portugal_en.pdf.

[88] See www.govtech.gov.pt.

A regulatory sandbox can allow open communication between innovators, market participants and regulators to negotiate the right balance of regulation to reduce risks while not stifling innovation. For blockchain applications, setting up sandboxes can reduce barriers to entry for firms, create a supportive network for innovation and improve the chances for successful implementation. Singapore has created the Smart Financial Center, where it has invested $225 million to develop fintech products in a sandbox environment. The sandbox allows the Monetary Authority of Singapore to develop financial technology applications in a controlled environment, where legal regulations are relaxed, that allows free experimentation with new products and services.[89]

B. CREATING THE REGULATORY ENVIRONMENT FOR SUPPORT BLOCKCHAIN INNOVATION WHILE ADDRESSING POTENTIAL RISKS

Blockchain comprises of multiple layers of governance that interact with each other in its operation. For example, the first layer is the Internet and its protocol (e.g., TCP/IP) and is followed by the actual blockchain layer (e.g., Ethereum) on which smart contracts and other applications are implemented.[90] However, only a small number of developers have the technical skills and legitimacy required to implement such changes and, therefore, changes are implemented in a non-democratic process by a small group of developers. Governance of blockchain is, therefore, a significant challenge as the decision-making process cannot only involve those who build the technology but must also include those who will ultimately use it and be affected by the decisions,[91] avoiding the potential scenario whereby only a handful of entities control blockchain technology becomes critical. Shared governance approaches can ensure that the perspectives of all who have a stake are considered, regardless of whether they are part of the sovereign decision-maker's geographic territory.[92]

Standardization in blockchain offers a form of light-touch self-regulating mechanism that may have benefits in terms of incentivizing innovation, benchmarking technological development and promoting economic growth.[93] Adoption of voluntary standards can play a role in ensuring interoperability and avoiding unnecessary bottlenecks, creating a common understanding and consensus as to ways to address issues surrounding security, privacy and resilience in relation to blockchain or reinforcing end-user trust in the technology. Proponents of this approach to regulation argue that it can create tentative, non-binding norms, thus a common vernacular in a new landscape whereby "harder" forms of legislation may stifle innovation or create barriers to entry. The assumption with the voluntary nature of standards is that the industry will converge towards the most optimal standard for the welfare of all stakeholders. However, standardization can also become an area of contention among innovators and technology users. To avoid such problems, the international standard setting must abide by a set of principles.[94]

While proponents of blockchain technology tend to advocate a voluntary arrangement of industry standardization, the pace of technological change inevitably brings challenges that are fundamental to the commercial organizations and the legal system entrusted to regulate the market. Such challenges relate to the end-users, the service providers and platforms. Therefore, the question is whether innovative technologies will result in innovative legal frameworks. This is a pressing question in China, where blockchain technology and smart contracts are increasingly being applied as e-commerce continues to expand. It is argued that, even though there is a gap in the existing regulatory framework, the current legal system can accommodate or mitigate legal risks presented by smart contracts. On the one hand, it is premature to change the existing legal framework in response to relatively new technology. However, the regulatory framework for platform operators needs to be adjusted to carefully incentivize them to diligently check and verify the information of vendors who conduct business on their platforms.

Despite the rapid advances in technology, many aspects of sophisticated commercial agreements are

[89] See https://www.mas.gov.sg/development/fintech/regulatory-sandbox.

[90] Vincent Mignon, 2019, Blockchains – Perspectives and Challenges, in Kraus, Obrist and Hari (eds.), *Blockchains, Smart Contracts, Decentralised Autonomous Organisations and the Law.*

[91] Marcella Atzori, 2015, Technology and Decentralized Governance: Is the State Still Necessary? 27: https://papers.ssrn.com/sol3/papers.cfm?abstract_id=2709713#:~:text=Marcella%20Atzori,-University%20College%20of&text=In%20particular%2C%20the%20paper%20verifies,and%20dismiss%20traditional%20central%20authorities.

[92] Vint Cerf, Patrick Ryan, Max Senges, 2014, Internet governance is our shared responsibility, *I/S: A Journal of Law and Policy for the Information Society, vol. 10(1):* https://papers.ssrn.com/sol3/papers.cfm?abstract_id=2309772.

[93] For recent developments in blockchain standardization, see International Organization for Standardization (ISO) Technical Committee (TC) 307 on *Blockchain and Distributed Ledger Technologies:* https://www.iso.org/committee/6266604.html.

[94] This is a topic covered by the Technical Barriers to Trade Committee of the World Trade Organization (WTO).

not subject to automation, including matters requiring human judgement, the rendition of sophisticated or human-intensive services, and the resolution of disputes. Therefore, the blockchain technology is incapable of dealing with relatively complex relational contracts due to the rigidity arising from codes as well as the structure of decentralization. Hence, despite the claim that intermediates will be eliminated due to the decentralized architecture and confidence in relationships enabled by blockchain technology, intermediaries will continue to play an important role, socially and legally. In terms of digital platforms, regulators need to stay alert to misconduct by platforms in their role as gatekeepers. Regulations should focus more on the duty of platforms to monitor and verify the information of their vendors.

Specific regulatory issues that arise with the implementation of blockchain are discussed below.

1. Privacy security and data protection

Like many web-based services operating worldwide, data protection rules of each jurisdiction in which users are concerned would apply for blockchain technology, for which the processing of personal data across geographical boundaries would be common practice. Different territorial jurisdictions may have different laws in place, with some taking the lead on shaping the future application of data protection, privacy, and security in relation to the blockchain. The General Data Protection Regulation (GDPR)[95] in the European Union (EU) is one such example and is the most advanced regulation at the supranational level and is likely to be the legal benchmark in privacy and data protection for the digital economy.

The key aspect of blockchain technology is that information is not stored in a single space but is distributed across various sites known as *nodes*. No centralized authority takes control of information processing, as this is done using consensus algorithm on a peer-to-peer structure known as the *distributed* ledger – which mitigates many risks that centralized ledgers faced. Unlike centralized ledgers which are stored in one single space, distributed ledgers cannot be destroyed, lost or altered, given that they are spread and replicated across multiple nodes.[96] In this regard, blockchain technology is viewed by some as solving the "single point of failure" issue. Under most current centralized IT systems where the processing of data is entrusted to one single entity, in the case of a cybersecurity breach such as hacking, the personal data can be altered or lost. Such issues are unlikely to occur when personal data is replicated across various locations in the blockchain system.[97] Transparency is also a key aspect of certain blockchain systems, where users may have a clearer understanding of how their personal data is used and by whom.

However, even with the most advanced data protection regulations, such as the GDPR, there are problems with identifying how each user of blockchain is categorized and, thus, how data protection laws may apply. For example, such problems can be seen when considering whether every blockchain user is a controller or a joint controller, or if data subjects automatically become data controllers too. This is important for determining the legal role and responsibility of each user of the technology. It would also be very difficult to identify and hold accountable all participants of large public blockchains.

Some believe that the public blockchain features are "on a collision course with the European Union privacy law" and incompatible at a conceptual level with privacy protection principles of the European Union General Data Protection Regulation (GDPR).[98]

The GDPR relies on the notion of a "controller" who is responsible for compliance with the GDPR.[99] In the current platform economy (with large intermediaries such as Google, Amazon etc.) it would be generally possible to identify the entity that is the controller. With a public blockchain, there would often be no central point of control.

As blockchain technology is set to disrupt existing business models, further consideration is needed on how best to regulate it. Without many concrete deployment cases available yet, it is difficult to foretell all impacts that blockchain may have on society, and therefore what exactly this regulation is likely to look like.

---

[95] Regulation (EU) 2016/679 of the European Parliament and of the Council of 27 April 2016 on the protection of natural persons with regard to the processing of personal data and on the free movement of such data.

[96] Adrien Alberini and Vincent Pfammatter, 2019, Blockchain and data protection, in Kraus et al. (eds.), 2019.

[97] Jacek Czarnecki, 2017, Blockchains and Personal Data Protection Regulations Explained, *Coindesk, 26 April, available at:* https://www.coindesk.com/blockchains-personal-data-protection-regulations-explained.

[98] Lokke Moerel, 2020, Blockchain and data protection, in DiMatteo et al. (eds.), *The Cambridge Handbook of Smart Contracts, Blockchain Technology and Digital Platforms.*

[99] The entity that, alone or jointly with others, determines the purpose and means of the data processing (Art. 4 GDPR).

2. Financial regulations

The constant evolution of crypto-based technologies being implemented in financial markets transactions is a complex issue for regulators to grasp both legally and practically. The absence of an international convention for regulating blockchain in financial markets, could potentially be problematic given the transnational nature of global finance, coupled with the fact that distributed ledger technology runs across borders.

The regulatory approach by different countries or jurisdictions varies considerably with respect to blockchain in financial markets. Some develop ad hoc regulations adapted to technology (e.g. Malta, Gibraltar (United Kingdom) and New York State (United States)), while others refer to existing regulations to apply to new activities (e.g. Switzerland). Meanwhile, a few countries have taken a more restrictive approach such as prohibiting certain blockchain-related investments (e.g. Algeria and the Plurinational State of Bolivia), while many other countries have so far not taken any position.

A key consideration is the need to prevent systemic risk vis-à-vis cryptocurrency and financial markets. If investors accumulate debt to purchase large sums of cryptocurrency using fiat money, and there is a devaluation in the exchange rate, this could lead to payment defaults in the respective fiat currency.[100] This systemic risk can, of course, be accentuated by speculative activities which create asset bubbles, as seen during the past decade with the Bitcoin cryptocurrency. For example, with blockchain technology, a person's bank record is replicated and synchronized across multiple sites so that no single entity takes control of maintaining a single version of the information.

Taxation is another regulatory issue which raises several questions that are treated with different tax jurisdictions, creating legal ambiguity. For tax purposes, the digital or virtual currencies that are encrypted using cryptography – known as tokens – are relevant for determining their scope and function, and whether the token entitles the owner to receive a payment from a third party. Questions arise as to whether miners (those that process transaction records in the ledger) receiving payment for their mining activities constitutes taxable income, or whether VAT should be applicable for mining services rendered. In the United States, the payment received from the mining of virtual currency must be considered taxable income.[101] Other countries such as Canada and Sweden take a similar approach but can differentiate tax treatment based on whether the mining is classified as a leisurely activity or a business activity. Another possibility is to consider a tax treatment that mirrors investments in shares or bonds.[102]

3. Intellectual property regulations

The relationship between blockchain and intellectual property (IP) rights can be viewed from two perspectives: from the developer end, and from the user end. The development of blockchain technology and blockchain-based applications, although largely based on open-source code, may be subject to various intellectual property rights. Copyright, patents and trademarks will play an important role in the consolidation or dissemination of the technology and could either potentially curb innovation by limiting access to newcomers or enable its diffusion. It is therefore important to consider how IP rights will most stimulate the use and development of new blockchain applications.

From the perspective of the user end, blockchain can serve the IP system in various ways, not only for the defensive protection of IP assets (i.e., for litigation, proving ownership rights, tracking original and counterfeit products, ensuring better revenue for authors/performers, etc.) but may also serve as a decentralized ledger for unregistered IP rights such as copyright works or for the European Union's design right. Smart contracts in blockchains also raise the prospect of eliminating or reducing the need for IP registration, which would not require the intervention of national or regional IP offices.

Blockchain already operates under the IP system, given that open source is based on copyright law, which allows for the widespread use of blockchain-based applications, allowing both developers and users to benefit from improvements made in the existing blockchain. The Bitcoin and Ethereum trademark and logos are also based on an open license and can be freely used by legitimate users such as business accepting payment in the cryptocurrency, thus enabling different players to enter markets.[103] Blockchain could potentially

[100] Biba Homsy, 2019, Aspects of Swiss financial regulation, in Kraus et al. (eds.), 2019.

[101] Internal Revenue Service (IRS) Publication No. 525, available at https://www.irs.gov/publications/p525.

[102] Thierry Obrist and Roland A. Pfister, 2019, Tax treatment of cryptocurrency holders and miners in the era of virtual currencies from a multijurisdictional and Swiss perspective, in Kraus et al. (eds.), 2019.

[103] Daniel Kraus and Charlotte Boulay, 2019, Blockchains: aspects of intellectual property law, in Kraus et al. (eds.), 2019.

help with IP management in technology transfer and commercialization, by allowing patent owners to find potential licensees for related know-how and trade secrets in connection to a patented invention.

However, blockchain can equally enable right holders to enact restrictive measures, which could negatively influence the development and use of blockchains, particularly if they were to be used for anticompetitive practices. There are also differences across different jurisdictions as to what can be protected under different forms of IP in blockchain technologies (e.g., the software can be patented in the United States but not the European Union), creating legal complexities between different geographical regions in which blockchains operate.

VI. INTERNATIONAL COLLABORATION

A. SHARING KNOWLEDGE AND INFORMATION AND CONDUCTING RESEARCH

The application of blockchain technology is a very recent phenomenon, and its long-term implications are not yet clear. Research forms the foundation for consensus building, policy advocacy and technical assistance activities. Several United Nations agencies have worked on research, policy analysis and data collection, both regarding potential economic and social impacts and policy and regulatory responses.

For example, UNCTAD has examined the impact of frontier technologies, including blockchain, in its 2018 and 2021 *Technology and Innovation Reports*, with the 2021 edition focusing on the impact on inequalities. It has also examined the status and trends of the digital economy and e-commerce in its *Digital Economy Reports*. WIPO has established the Blockchain Task Force under the Committee on WIPO Standards (CWS) to explore the possibility of using blockchain technology in the processes of providing intellectual property (IP) rights protection and prepare a proposal for a new WIPO standard supporting the potential application of blockchain technology within the IP ecosystem. To support the activities of the Task Force, WIPO Secretariat is developing a Blockchain whitepaper for IP ecosystem, which is exploring the impact and potential use cases of the blockchain technology in the IP space. ESCAP has been observing, reviewing, collecting, and documenting examples in the region of where blockchain technology has had the biggest developmental impact. ESCAP has strengthened the awareness of network through the delivery of several policy sessions at the Global Forum on Human Settlements in Bangkok in September 2019, Seventh Asia Pacific Urban Forum (APUF7) in Jakarta in October 2019, and through the expert group meetings (water cycles and the blockchain technology for sustainable development in June 2019).

The Commission on Science and Technology for Development of the United Nations could consider the following areas for strengthening international collaboration:

(a) **Coordinate awareness-raising.** The Commission could coordinate the international community's efforts to raise awareness on challenges and opportunities of blockchain innovation, sharing successful examples on the use of blockchain technology for sustainable development with countries that are late to integrate the technology to their innovation ecosystem. It is critical for the international community to continue to compile, analyse and disseminate information about these cases to raise awareness and inform the application of blockchain for sustainable development.

(b) **Blockchain Innovation Strategy Assessments.** UNCTAD, as the secretariat of the Commission, and in collaboration with other agencies of the United Nations system, could conduct research and analysis focused on innovation system, policy and regulatory frameworks in developing countries for harnessing blockchain innovation for sustainable development. This can be done by taking stock of the potential for innovation and diversification into sectors that are at the core of the blockchain innovation ecosystem. Technical support could be provided through workshops or country-specific blockchain innovation strategy assessments. The findings of these studies could be discussed at the Commission to raise awareness and build a common understanding of the international cooperation for harnessing blockchain for sustainable development.

B. HELPING TO SET GUIDELINES, NORMS AND STANDARDS

As discussed in chapter IV, the adoption of blockchain technology has unintended consequences related to privacy and security. These two points are issues that are at stake with the blockchain technology and need recommendations on regulation from international organizations. As the potential implications are becoming clearer to Governments, there is a growing need for policy guidance, training, global regulation, and standard-setting to guarantee a fair and responsible adoption of the technology in developing countries.

In this regard, the United Nations/CEFACT, alongside its advisory group on advanced technologies, is looking at developing a blockchain-based environment/framework in which trustworthy, common identification and communication interchange is facilitated. This aims at creating a trustworthy context for Blockchain to enhance its benefits and reduce risks. United Nations/CEFACT is looking at developing interoperability of message exchange to promote a global regulation and framework for blockchain, enabling blockchain to fully deploy its benefits for all the Sustainable Development Goals under the 2030 Agenda, while minimizing the risks. United Nations/CEFACT created the United Nations/ CEFACT Standards and UNECE Recommendations to provide a global basis for interoperable semantic data exchange, including UNECE Recommendation on Single Window and Recommendation on Single Submission Portals (SSPs) together with over 200 UN/ CEFACT data exchange standards of United Nations/ EDIFACT UNSMs and the United Nations/CEFACT Reference Data Model subset XML Schemas, which are based on the United Nations/CEFACT Core Component Library (CCL). These include the Electronic Sanitary and Phytosanitary Certificate (eCERT) schemas, the Electronic Consignment Note (e-CMR) schema.

Based on this example, the international community could consider:

(a) **Promote the development of standards,** recommendations and regulations. The international community should promote the development of standards, recommendations and regulations on blockchain, to harness its potential, including promoting privacy and security. This can also be done through studies, reports, white papers and any other relevant documentation.

(b) **Intergovernmental consensus-building.** The Commission on Science and Technology for Development could play an essential role in promoting international best practices, international guidelines and legal frameworks governing the blockchain. The impact could be maximized by building and strengthening collaboration ties with existent initiatives of the United Nations system.

C. HELPING BUILD THE CAPACITY OF GOVERNMENTS TO PLAY ITS ROLE IN THE BLOCKCHAIN ECOSYSTEM, INCLUDING IN TERMS OF OVERSIGHT CAPABILITIES

Governments and regulators in developing countries would face many challenges in designing and implementing the required institutional changes that would be needed to harness blockchain innovation for sustainable development while reducing risks. They usually have low capacity and resources to keep abreast of the developments in the technology and the innovation ecosystem. International organizations should support these governments, particularly in low- and lower-middle-income developing countries, including the least developed countries, in building their national capacities in engaging with blockchain innovation and promoting the required institutional change.

In this regard, UNCTAD assists developing countries, in particular LDCs, LLDCs and SIDS, to address the challenges and opportunities in relation to innovation strategies, trade facilitation and e-commerce and to develop their international trade capacities. To this end, UNCTAD offers a range of technical cooperation and capacity-building activities for which it would be worthwhile exploring the integration of components on the blockchain, such as UNCTAD *STI Policy Reviews*, *Empowerment Programme for National Trade Facilitation Committees*, the *Rapid eTrade Readiness Assessments, E-commerce, and Law Reform Programme* and the *ICT Policy Reviews*.

UNIDO has developed a methodological framework to assess the readiness of a commodity value chain to adopt blockchain technology. The objective of the methodology is to address a general approach to assess a value chain from a data-sharing perspective and to go into the specific requirements that come with implementing blockchain technology. The methodology has been set up in such a way that it can be applied to assess the feasibility and readiness to adopt blockchain for any commodity value chain from any sourcing country.

ESCWA has explored the potentials of Blockchain technologies on the provision of its services to member countries within its mandate related to social and economic affairs. For example, ESCWA is considering the use of Blockchain technologies in managing COVID-19 in airports in partnership with the International Chamber of Commerce and OakPass. Some Arab countries (ESCWA member States) have been considering several applications of Blockchain in their development processes as well. Additionally, ESCWA has been exploring the provision of member States with policy advice and policy support in this area.

UNECE has an active project focusing on enhancing transparency and traceability in the garment and footwear sector through blockchain. It has been proven by UNECE experts that brands only have a limited overview of their value chains. Only around 34 per cent of fashion companies implement tracking and tracing in their supply chain, and companies usually only have control or overview of the value chain process that does not go further than the manufacturing and assembling of the product (UNECE study, 2019). UNECE, alongside its partners (ILO and ITC), is launching a pilot to create a digital identity for a cotton shirt by connecting it to sustainability certificates. It is proven that the cotton sector has major environmental and social impacts, which are higher than for other textile fibres.[104]

The international community could consider the following recommendation to strengthen international cooperation in this area:

(a) **Training programmes.** The international community could contribute to developing content-specific training programmes for countries and institutions planning to implement a blockchain-related solution to provide them with relevant information about the technologies' capabilities and limitations.

(b) **Know-how transfer programmes.** The international communities can execute complementary know-how transfer programmes (including applied training programmes or projects in executing the transformation of a country's public service applications with blockchain technology) that allow engaging ecosystem actors with pioneer countries and less developed ecosystem owning countries.

(c) **Decision-making tools.** Similarly, the international community could support Governments with decision-making tools to invest or not to invest in new technologies and increase the preparedness countries to adopt and adapt new technologies.

D. USING BLOCKCHAIN IN UNITED NATIONS OPERATIONS

The United Nations system started to develop projects based on blockchain technology very recently. In the past three years, a few projects have been implementing in many of the various applications allowed by the blockchain technology.

- Public registry: UN-Habitat has implemented a system to record land ownership in a digital registry which can then serve as the basis for other government services such as urban planning, citizen engagement and revenue generation.[105]
- Supply chain tracking: UNDP is piloting a system where the purchaser of a chocolate bar receives an impact token which can be sent back directly to the cocoa farmer to expand its cocoa tree plantation or for the consumer to be used as a discount on other products.[106]
- Digital finance: WFP and UN-Women have used blockchain in refugee camps to track cash entitlements that are disbursed to the people WFP serves. Cash value from WFP is stored in an 'account' for individual recipients and is maintained on the blockchain. That cash can be spent on goods and services from approved retailers. The transactions are recorded in a blockchain where the identity of refugees is secured with the existing biometric authentication technology of UNHCR. WFP has a record of every transaction. This not only saves on financial transaction fees in the camp setting but ensures greater security and privacy for Syrian refugees. The project currently coordinates the delivery of food assistance for over 100,000 Syrian refugees.[107] UNICEF has used smart contract in Kazakhstan to streamline processes related to cash transfers between UNICEF and its implementing partners on the ground. It also improved the transparency and accountability of partnerships and related transfers of resources. The platform has allowed for streamlined verification of the results achieved by partners and allowed the blockchain-based smart contract to release the payment automatically after verification and authorisation. It has showcased how smart contracts can be used to expedite the processing of paperwork and payment.[108]
- CryptoFund: UNICEF built its own cryptocurrency-fund, called the CryptoFund which makes investments into startups in the form of bitcoin or ether. By providing funding in the form of cryptocurrency, there is the transparency of where funds come from, where they are invested and where the investees use their funds. Bitcoin and ether allow the transfers to take place in a few seconds, regardless of where the

[104] See http://www.unece.org/tradewelcome/traceability-for-sustainable-garment-and-footwear.html.

[105] See https://reliefweb.int/report/afghanistan/city-all-investing-sustainable-urbanization-afghanistan.

[106] See https://www.fastcompany.com/90413242/this-new-blockchain-chocolate-bar-is-brought-to-you-by-the-un.

[107] See https://innovation.wfp.org/project/building-blocks.

[108] See https://www.unicef.org/innovation/blockchain/digicus.

investees are around the world. This new asset class allows UNICEF to leverage a new donation type.[109] UNIDO has leveraged blockchain in a Sustainable Development Goal accelerator fund to streamline financial opportunities to the advantage of SMEs moving towards the circular economy. The project uses blockchain to conduct impact investment verification activities. The project has been recently renamed as Sustainable Development Goal Impact Investment Platform (SIIP) and is currently under review.[110]

- Sustainability Map: In 2019, ITC explored using blockchain technology to improve visualization of transparency, traceability and accountability on voluntary sustainability standards. ITC used its Sustainability Map tool, which helps businesses, regardless of their position in value chains, chart their part toward more sustainable trade as a transparency and traceability platform. The purpose of the pilot initiative was to visualize blockchain-based supply chain traceability data from multiple companies and sources, to support a culture of transparency and mutual accountability across global networks while providing consumers with the sustainability information they demand.[111]

Agencies in the United Nations system have also established networks to share experiences and information on the implementation of solutions using blockchain. The United Nations Innovation Network (UNIN) has set up a Blockchain Group to raise awareness within the United Nations system and share experiences in the implementation of applications using blockchain technology including related to cash and remittance transfers, supply chain tracking, record keeping, digital identity and increasing transparency.[112] The Atrium is a platform that focusses on encouraging cooperation between United Nations agencies by stimulating learning and knowledge transfer of both IP and experience between United Nations staff members interested in blockchain technology. An underlying private permission blockchain has been set up to enable the use of Remix – a smart contract development and deployment tool – and provision of tokens via the Bounties platform – which allow for the creation of micro-tasks incentivized through a token.[113]

The United Nations Centre for Trade Facilitation and e-business (United Nations/CEFACT) – a subsidiary body of the UNECE – is running a United Nations inter-agency round table called "Blockchain for the Sustainable Development Goals" in the aim to update each United Nations organization on the ongoing work with regards to DTL as well as share know-how. This project has been ongoing since the month of May 2019 and groups organizations, such as the [Sustainable Development Goal] SDG Lab, UNECE, IOM, ITC, ITU, JIU, UNAIDS, UNCTAD, UPU, WFP, WHO, WIPO and WTO. Sharing updates on the work each other and know-how mean that the intention is to seek to understand the full possible implementation of blockchain to realize every Sustainable Development Goal of the 2030 Agenda.

As a way forward, the United Nations and the international community could consider:

(a) **Continue exploring the use of blockchain in projects implemented by the United Nations system:** The United Nations system could continue to invest in blockchain solutions for their operations involving data protection, authentications and certification. This is paramount as it involves not only technical initiatives but legislation and regulations to pace up with the breakthroughs stemming in the blockchain.

(b) **Establish a partnership's framework:** The United Nations could facilitate the establishment of a framework to encourage partnerships to capitalize on the use of blockchain for development, for example, to lay the foundation for the inclusive digital economy in the developing regions.

(c) **Share know-how and experiences:** The international community should create inter-agency meetings to share know-how, experiences and ways forward to realize the Sustainable Development Goals through blockchain. The international community should look at existing and developing standards, recommendations, regulations to explain blockchain, harness its potential and promote its privacy and security. This can also be done through studies, reports, white papers and any other relevant documentation.

---

[109] See https://www.unicef.org/press-releases/unicef-launches-cryptocurrency-fund.

[110] UNIDO, 2019, SIIP: Enabling private financing of SMEs to facilitate more circular business models, available at https://www.unido.org/siip (accessed on 8 April 2020).

[111] Contribution from ITC, available at https://unctad.org/system/files/non-official-document/CSTD_2020-21_c14_B_ITC_en.pdf.

[112] See https://www.uninnovation.network/blockchain.

[113] Contribution from WFP, available at https://unctad.org/system/files/non-official-document/CSTD_2020-21_c41_B_WFP_en.pdf.

ANNEX

BLOCKCHAIN GLOSSARY

Concepts	*Definition*
	A
Altcoin	Altcoin (short for 'alternative coin') is any cryptocurrency other than Bitcoin. Many altcoins are forks [see below for definition] of Bitcoin with minor changes; there are hundreds of altcoins being traded around the world: Litecoin, Monero, and Dash.
51% Attack	This concept describes the situation in which more than half of the blockchain network's power is controlled by a single entity or group, this entity or group can manipulate it on purpose or conduct conflicting transactions that can compromise the system.
ASIC – Application Specific Integrated Circuit	An ASIC is a silicon chip designed specifically for a certain task. In the world of blockchain, ASIC usually refers to chips developed to run on mining computers and is considered superior to CPUs and GPUs due to its capacity to significant electrical power savings.
	B
Bitcoin	Bitcoin is the first decentralized, open-source cryptocurrency that runs on a global peer-to-peer network, without the need for a centralized issuer. Bitcoin was created in 2009 by Satoshi Nakomoto – a pseudonym for an individual whose real identity is unknown – and the concept of cryptocurrency was outlined in a white paper titled "Bitcoin: A Peer-to-Peer Electronic Cash System". Bitcoin is the first real-world application of blockchain.
Block	Blocks are packages of data that carry permanently and digitally recorded data on the blockchain network.
Blockchain	Blockchain is a cryptographic protocol that allows separate parties to increase the trustworthiness of a transaction, it is comprised blocks (see above for definition), and each block is "chained" to the next block using a cryptographic signature. This allows blockchains to act like a ledger (see below for definition), which can be shared with and accessed by anyone with the appropriate permissions. Some examples of blockchain-based cryptocurrencies are Bitcoin, Litecoin, Monero and Dash, to name a few.
	C
Cryptocurrency	A cryptocurrency is a digital currency based on mathematics and uses encryption techniques to regulate the creation of units of currency as well as verifying the transfer of funds. It is designed to operate independently of a central bank, with each token (see below for definition) and transaction uniquely encrypted.
Crypto-fiat currency	Crypto-fiat currency is a digital currency issued and governed by national central banks.
	D
DAO – Decentralized Autonomous Organization	This concept describes an organization whose decisions are made electronically by written computer code and manage itself without the need for a central authority.
DeFi – Decentralized finance	DeFi refers to the economic paradigm shift enabled by decentralized technologies, particularly blockchain networks. DeFi represents a shift from a centralized and closed financial system to a universally accessible economy that is based on open protocols that are interoperable, programmable and composable.
DLT – distributed ledger technology	DLT refers to the practice that uses nodes (see below for definition) to record, share and synchronize transactions in their respective electronic ledgers (instead of keeping data centralized as in a traditional ledger). The participant at each node of the network can access the recordings shared across that network and can own an identical copy of it. Any changes or additions made to the ledger are reflected and copied to all participants in a matter of seconds or minutes.

Concepts	*Definition*
	E
Ethereum	Ethereum is a blockchain-based decentralized platform for applications featuring smart contracts (see below for definition) functionality. It is aimed at solving issues associated with censorship, fraud, and third-party interference. Ethereum is the second-largest cryptocurrency platform by market capitalization, behind Bitcoin. Ethereum provides a decentralized virtual machine, the Ethereum Virtual Machine (EVM), which can execute scripts using an international network of public nodes. Ethereum was proposed in late 2013 by Vitalik Buterin, a cryptocurrency researcher and programmer.
Ether (ETH)	Ether is the cryptocurrency generated by Ethereum miners as a reward for computations performed to secure the blockchain. Ether functions as a fuel of the Ethereum ecosystem by acting as a medium of incentive and form of payment for network participants to execute essential operations.
	F
Fiat currency	Fiat currency is government-issued currency (instrument of exchange, store of value and unit of account) whose value is not backed by a physical commodity, such as gold or silver, but rather by the Government that issued it. The value of fiat currency is derived from the relationship between supply and demand and the stability of the issuing Government. Most modern paper currencies are fiat currencies, such as the United states dollar and the euro.
Fork	A fork creates an alternative version of a blockchain and is often enacted intentionally to apply upgrades to a network. Since blockchain is decentralized, each change to the network has to be accepted by its users in order to go through. If enough users accept an upgrade or code change, it is rolled out across the network. A change which still recognizes and supports older versions of the blocks is called a soft fork, while one which makes it backwards incompatible (not compatible with older versions) is called a hard fork, thus requiring all participants to upgrade to the new version in order to be able to continue participating on the network.
	H
Hash	Hash is the practice that takes an input, and then outputs an alphanumeric string known as the "hash value" or "digital fingerprint". Each block in the blockchain contains the hash value that validated the transaction before it followed by its own hash value. Hashes confirm transactions on the blockchain.
	L
Ledger	A digital log of all of the transactions which took place on a certain blockchain network. Copies of the ledger are stored across the network and are constantly updated to match each other so that transactions can be verified by all participants on the network.
	M
Mining	Mining is a peer-to-peer computer process of allocating computer power to carry out transactions on the network and being rewarded with tokens (see below for definition). Cryptocurrency mining is the digital equivalent of a miner striking gold in the ground – while digging in a sandbox. Each transaction is encrypted by complex computational math problems which require significant computing power to be processed. Miners who solve the computational math problems first, thus enabling the transaction to take place are rewarded with cryptocurrency payments.
	N
Natural asset tokens	Natural assets represent the global stockpile of natural resources, such as gold, oil, gas or even carbon and water. Natural asset tokens represent the value of these tangible goods in peer-to-peer markets with a real-time settlement.
Node	A node is a system on the network that operates a full copy of validated transactions of the blockchain ledger (see above for definition). Any computer connected to the blockchain network is referred to as a node. In some blockchains, such as Bitcoin and Ethereum, all nodes participate in the consensus process, in others, it may be only be selected nodes.

Concepts	*Definition*
	P
Peer-to-peer	Peer-to-peer (P2P) refers to the decentralized interactions between two or more parties in a highly interconnected network. Participants of a P2P network deal directly with each other through a single mediation point.
Private key	A private key is a digital code known only to the user and could be equated with a password. Each participant on the network holds a private key.
Proof of stake	Proof of stake is a consensus distribution algorithm which determines which users are eligible to add new blocks (see above for definition) to the blockchain, thus, earning a cryptocurrency payment as mining fee. Using this method, of the users who participate in the mining process, those with more tokens are favoured over those with less.
Proof of work	Preceding proof of stake, proof of work is a consensus distribution algorithm used to decide which user is eligible to create a new block (see above for definition]. However, with the proof of work method, eligibility is determined by computing power and not by the miners' digital wealth.
Public key	A public key is a digital code obtained and used by anyone to encrypt messages before they are sent to a known recipient with a matching private key for decryption. The public key encrypts a message into an unreadable format, and the corresponding private key makes it readable again for the intended party; therefore, no intermediary is required.
	S
Security token	A security token is a type of digital asset that represents its value from some other external tradable asset. Security tokens can both represent real-life material assets, such as square meters of real estate or grams of gold and non-material assets, such as companies' shares. Therefore, the security token provides the rights of ownership over a part of a company and can be traded peer-to-peer without financial intermediaries. The process of generating security tokens is called a security token offering (STO), which is a type of fundraising that is performed with a company offering tokenized securities.
Shard	A shard is a horizontal partition of data in a database or network. Each shard is held on a separate database server to spread workload with the purpose of scalability, enabling the network to process more transactions at the same time.
Stablecoin	Stablecoin is any cryptocurrency whose value is pegged to a stable asset, such as fiat currency (see above for definition) or gold. Therefore, a stablecoin is an asset that offers price stability characteristics as it is measured against a known amount of an asset not subject to high fluctuation.
Smart contract	Smart contracts are the second-generation blockchains. While Bitcoin only records monetary transactions of ownership of the cryptocurrency, second-generation blockchains expand it to incorporate programming languages allowing for more customizable transactions. These smart contracts consist of all the clauses and conditions that are transparent to all nodes, when the terms of a smart contract are met, the contract will be automatically executed, with the participating parties being rewarded according to the contract's terms. Therefore, this second generation of blockchain turns the blockchain into a programmable protocol that can operate more than the cash-like tokens transactions allowing other financial instruments, such as loans or bonds, to be represented. Some platforms run based on smart contracts are Ethereum, Ethereum Classic, NEO and QTUM, to name a few.

Concepts	Definition
T	
Token	A token is a unit of value related to a specific blockchain network, representing its currency, giving value to transactions within the network. For example, the Bitcoin network's token is called BTC, and the Litecoin network's token is called LTC.
Timestamp server	A timestamp server works by taking a hash (see above for definition) of a block of items to be timestamped and widely publishing the hash across the blockchain. The timestamp proves that the data must have existed at the time in order to get into the hash. Each timestamp includes the previous timestamp in its hash, forming a chain, with each additional timestamp reinforcing the ones before it.
Turing-completeness	Turing machines can compute precisely the class of problems that can be solved algorithmically. A system of data-manipulation rules such as a programming language is said to be Turing-complete or computationally universal if it can be used to simulate any Turing machine. Therefore, Turing-completeness refers to a system of data-manipulation rules that, given enough time and memory along with the necessary instructions, can solve any computational problem.
U	
Utility tokens	A utility token is a digital asset that grants the owner of the token (see above for definition) a specific right in the usage of a company's products like being first to access it or getting other privileges. The major difference between security tokens and utility tokens is in the intended use and functionality of the tokens. Utility tokens do not provide the rights of ownership over a part of a company; therefore, utility tokens are not created to be an investment. Blockchain offers a platform that can be used to create a voting system that allows investors to exercise control over the company's decision-making process. Utility tokens are not intended to give their holders the ability to control how decisions are made in a company; instead, they help companies to gain funding without losing their independence. Utility tokens are often used for Initial Coin Offerings (ICO).

REFERENCES

Ackermann J and Meier M (2018). Blockchain 3.0: the next generation of blockchain systems. *Proceedings of Advanced Seminar Blockchain Technologies (Advanced Seminar Blockchain Technologies).*

Akilo D (2018). The emergence of blockchain as a service providers. Available at https://businessblockchainhq.com/blockchain-trends/the-emergence-of-blockchain-as-a-service-providers/ (accessed 30 January 2020).

Allen DWE, Berg A and Markey-Towler B (2018). Blockchain and supply chains: V-form organisations, value redistributions, de-commoditisation and quality proxies. *The Journal of The British Blockchain Association*. 2(1):1–8, The British Blockchain Association.

Anwar H (2019). Blockchain as a service: enterprise-grade BaaS solutions. Available at https://101blockchains.com/blockchain-as-a-service/ (accessed 30 January 2020).

Arup (2018). Becoming water wise through blockchain technology - Arup. (accessed 13 October 2020).

Bank of England (2014). The economics of digital currencies. Available at https://www.bankofengland.co.uk/-/media/boe/files/digital-currencies/the-economics-of-digital-currencies (accessed 22 October 2020).

BCRA (2020). Measures that guarantee foreign exchange for economic recovery. Available at https://www.bcra.gob.ar/Noticias/medidas-bcra-garantizan-divisas-para-recuperacion-economica-.asp (accessed 22 September 2020).

BIS (2020). Annual Economic Report. Available at https://www.bis.org/publ/arpdf/ar2020e.pdf.

Blockcerts (2020). Blockchain Credentials. Available at http://blockcerts.org/ (accessed 14 October 2020).

Bodkhe U et al. (2020). Blockchain for Industry 4.0: a comprehensive review. *IEEE Access*. 879764–79800.

Buterin V (2013). A next generation smart contract and decentralized application platform. Available at https://blockchainlab.com/pdf/Ethereum_white_paper-a_next_generation_smart_contract_and_decentralized_application_platform-vitalik-buterin.pdf (accessed 10 October 2020).

Carter T (2020). How blockchain can address wealth inequality. Available at https://thomascarter.io/how-blockchain-can-address-wealth-inequality/ (accessed 6 October 2020).

Chainalysis (2020). The chainalysis 2020 crypto crime report. Available at https://go.chainalysis.com/2020-Crypto-Crime-Report.html (accessed 2 October 2020).

Cheong W (2020). Here are all the ways bitcoin could help address income inequality in the 2020s. Available at https://www.businessinsider.com/this-is-how-bitcoin-can-end-income-inequality-in-2020 (accessed 6 October 2020).

CoinDesk (2014). Bitcoin pizza day: celebrating the pizzas bought for 10,000 BTC May. Available at https://www.coindesk.com/bitcoin-pizza-day-celebrating-pizza-bought-10000-btc (accessed 11 October 2020).

CoinMarketCap (2020). Cryptocurrency Prices, Charts And Market Capitalizations. Available at https://coinmarketcap.com/ (accessed 15 October 2020).

Commbank (2019). Blockchain "BioTokens" create new marketplace for biodiversity. Available at https://www.commbank.com.auhttps://www.commbank.com.au/guidance/newsroom/blockchain-biotokens-biodiversity-marketplace-201908.html (accessed 13 October 2020).

ConsenSys Codefi (2020). ConsenSys Q2 2020 DeFi Report. Available at https://consensys.net/insights/q2-2020-defi-report/ (accessed 10 October 2020).

Desjardins J (2020). Visual Capitalist. Available at https://www.visualcapitalist.com/all-of-the-worlds-money-and-markets-in-one-visualization-2020/ (accessed 8 October 2020).

Ethereum (2020). Ethereum 2.0 (Eth2). Available at https://ethereum.org (accessed 7 October 2020).

Ethereum Foundation (2020). Available at https://ethereum.foundation/ (accessed 7 October 2020).

Ethereum: Gas and fees (2020). Ethereum: Gas and fees. Available at https://ethereum.org (accessed 7 October 2020).

Ethereum Virtual Machine (EVM) (2020). Ethereum Virtual Machine (EVM). Available at https://ethereum.org/en/developers/docs/evm/ (accessed 7 October 2020).

Gaur V and Gaiha A (2020). Building a transparent supply chain. Available at https://hbr.org/2020/05/building-a-transparent-supply-chain (accessed 16 October 2020).

Graham FD (1940). The primary functions of money and their consummation in monetary policy. *The American Economic Review*. 30(1):1–16, American Economic Association.

Grand View Research (2019). Blockchain technology market worth $57,641.3 million by 2025. Available at https://www.grandviewresearch.com/press-release/global-blockchain-technology-market (accessed 30 January 2020).

Haig S (2020). Cointelegraph. Available at https://cointelegraph.com/news/coca-cola-embraces-dlt-and-ethereum-for-supply-chain-efficiency (accessed 27 October 2020).

Hayek FA (1976). Denationalization of Money, 1976. *First published by the Institute of Economic Affairs. London.*

IDC (2019). Worldwide blockchain spending forecast to reach $2.9 billion in 2019, according to new IDC spending guide. Available at https://www.idc.com/getdoc.jsp?containerId=prUS44898819 (accessed 30 January 2020).

Jevons WS (1876). *Money and the Mechanism of Exchange*. D. Appleton.

Jose A and Lanz D (2020). Argentina's new dollar tax is a boon for cryptocurrency. Available at https://decrypt.co/42215/argentinas-new-dollar-tax-boon-cryptocurrency-dai (accessed 19 September 2020).

Kamath R (2018). Food traceability on blockchain: Walmart's pork and mango pilots with IBM. Available at https://www.researchgate.net/publication/326188675_Food_Traceability_on_Blockchain_Walmart's_Pork_and_Mango_Pilots_with_IBM (accessed 16 October 2020).

MarketWatch (2019). Blockchain market size analytical overview, demand, trends and forecast to 2024. Available at https://www.marketwatch.com/press-release/blockchain-market-size-analytical-overview-demand-trends-and-forecast-to-2024-2019-04-05 (accessed 30 January 2020).

Nakamoto S (2008). Bitcoin: a peer-to-peer electronic cash system. Available at https://bitcoin.org/bitcoin.pdf (accessed 20 September 2020).

Oberhauser D (2019). Blockchain for environmental governance: can smart contracts reinforce payments for ecosystem services in Namibia? *Frontiers in Blockchain*. 2, Frontiers.

Patrizio A (2018). The top 10 blockchain as a service providers. Available at https://www.datamation.com/data-center/top-10-blockchain-as-a-service-providers.html (accessed 30 January 2020).

Perez C (2002). *Technological Revolutions and Financial Capital: The Dynamics of Bubbles and Golden Ages*. Edward Elgar Pub. Cheltenham.

Schmidt CG and Wagner SM (2019). Blockchain and supply chain relations: a transaction cost theory perspective. *Journal of Purchasing and Supply Management*. 25(4):100552.

Schumpeter JA (1939). *Business Cycles: A Theoretical, Historical, and Statistical Analysis of the Capitalist Process*. Martino Pub.

Sève MDL, Mason N and Nassiry D (2018). Delivering blockchain's potential for environmental sustainability. Available at https://www.odi.org/publications/11206-delivering-blockchain-s-potential-environmental-sustainability (accessed 20 October 2020).

Toti B (2020). Coin Journal. Available at https://coinjournal.net/news/ethereum-price-eth-usd-eyes-400-as-miner-fees-hit-new-highs/ (accessed 29 October 2020).

Tuwiner J (2020). 11 Major companies who accept Bitcoin - Where to apend Bitcoins. Available at https://www.buybitcoinworldwide.com/who-accepts-bitcoin/ (accessed 11 October 2020).

United Nations Innovation Network (2019). A Practical Guide to Using Blockchain within the United Nation. Available at https://www.uninnovation.network/blockchain (accessed 20 October 2020).

UN-Women (2018). From where I stand: Using blockchain technology to empower women. Available at https://www.unwomen.org/news/stories/2018/2/from-where-i-stand-olivier-mukuta (accessed 13 October 2020).

United Nations/CEFACT (2020). White paper blockchain in trade facilitation. Available at http://www.unece.org/fileadmin/DAM/cefact/GuidanceMaterials/WhitePaperBlockchain.pdf (accessed 20 October 2020).

Visa (2018). Visa fact sheet. Available at https://usa.visa.com/dam/VCOM/download/corporate/media/visanet-technology/aboutvisafactsheet.pdf (accessed 20 October 2020).

Waters R (2016). 'Ether' brought to earth by theft of $50m in cryptocurrency. Available at https://www.ft.com/content/591518a0-34df-11e6-ad39-3fee5ffe5b5b (accessed 7 October 2020).

WHO (2017). A study on the public health and socioeconomic impact of substandard and falsified medical products. Available at https://www.who.int/medicines/regulation/ssffc/publications/se-study-sf/en/ (accessed 24 October 2020).

Wildlife Credits (2020). An incentive to conserve. Available at https://wildlifecredits.com/node (accessed 14 October 2020).

Wood DG (2020). Ethereum: a secure decentralised generalised transaction ledger. Available at https://gavwood.com/paper.pdf (accessed 26 November 2020).